DATE DUE

Families Like Mine

Families Like Mine

Children of Gay Parents
Tell It Like It Is

Abigail Garner

HarperCollins*Publishers*

FIRST EDITION

Designed by Joseph Rutt

Printed on acid-free paper

Library of Congress Cataloging-in-Publication Data
Garner, Abigail.
    Families like mine : children of gay parents tell it like it is / Abigail Garner.—1st ed.
        p.   cm.
    ISBN 0-06-052757-9
    1.Children of gay parents. I. Title.

HQ777.8.G37 2004
306.874'086'64—dc22   2003056975

04 05 06 07 08 ❖/RRD 10 9 8 7 6 5 4 3 2 1

For my brother Ben
It was a joy growing up with you.

For Stefan Lynch
Thank you for your trailblazing.

For the sons and daughters
You inspire me every day.

Contents

"I truly believe that if we put the strength of our hearts and minds together we can change prejudice and my generation will grow up appreciating the glorious rainbow of diversity."

SOL KELLEY-JONES

Families Like Mine

Prologue
Some of My
Best Parents Are Gay

"That's clever," the middle-aged stranger told me when he read aloud the slogan on my homemade T-shirt. "'Some of my best friends are gay.' I like it."

"Actually," I said, pulling the front taut so he could read it more closely, "it doesn't say 'friends.' It says 'parents.' Some of my best *parents* are gay."

"Your *parents* are gay? How does that work?"

"My father and his partner are gay. My mom is straight. Some of my best parents are gay."

"Man," he said, shaking his head, "things you just don't think about."

This conversation took place in 1998 at the Twin Cities Pride Festival, an annual weekend that brings together over 100,000 people from lesbian, gay, bisexual, and transgender (LGBT) communities. Yet even in that crowd, the idea of gay parents—particularly parents who have adult children—remained a curious thing.

In my midtwenties, going to pride celebrations had become an increasingly lonely experience. I tried to understand why I was drawn to Pride and began to doubt if I really belonged there. Was I part of the community or not? I knew there had to be other adult children, but where were they? My T-shirt was a signal for them to come up to me and say, "Me, too!" I envisioned creating a group large enough to make us visible at Pride and everywhere else.

It was another two years before I was able to make the necessary connections. I began writing a column about LGBT families in a Minneapolis queer publication. I was confident that sons and daughters of LGBT parents were following the column because like me, they probably had not outgrown their habit of reading queer community publications. Within a matter of months after my debut column, I was delighted to receive "Me, too!" e-mails from teens and adult children who were just as thrilled to find me as I was to find them.

By June 2000, there was enough of a local network to march in the Pride parade. We revived my slogan from the homemade T-shirt, and ordered some that were made professionally. There were twenty-five of us; a mass of periwinkle shirts, carrying signs like I LOVE MY GAY DAD and ALTERNATIVE INSEMINATION BABY—ALL GROWN UP. We giggled at the perplexed expressions on people's faces as they read our banner: CHILDREN OF LESBIANS AND GAYS EVERYWHERE. Most parade watchers are now accustomed to the ever-growing brigade of strollers that LGBT parents push down the street every year, but few people put much thought into what happens to the children after they are potty-trained.

Yet even though we thought we had clearly and unmistakably identified ourselves, some people still didn't understand who we were. One man came up to me, checkbook in hand, ready to buy a T-shirt.

"Do you have gay parents?" I asked him.

"Oh, yeah!" he said. "I have a whole bunch!" When I asked about his family, it turned out that by "parents" he did not mean the people who raised him. He was a teacher referring to the parents of students in his classroom. After I explained for whom the T-shirts were intended, he said, "Oh! You have gay *parents*! You mean it *literally*!"

Yes. I mean it literally.

I was five years old when I found out my dad was gay. Since then the mention of my gay father or his partner, even in small talk, has turned almost every conversation into a lesson on gay families as I answer people's questions: *How did you find out? How did your mom react? Are you gay, too?*

Some of the questions I am asked are accusatory and doubt the competency of my father as a parent: *How could your dad choose his "lifestyle" over his wife? Is it true that gay parents molest their children? Did your father try to make you gay?*

Questions like these made me realize that the reality of my family and the common assumptions about families like mine were vastly different. When queer families remain hidden and mysterious, curious people tend to make up answers to their own questions with worst-case scenarios—scenarios fueled by prejudice and homophobia. I discovered that each time I mentioned the mundane details of my everyday life—going to the movies with my father and his partner, or washing the dishes together—I challenged people's stereotypes about gay parents, and gay people in general.

Even though I talked about my family when people asked, much of the time I avoided bringing attention to it in the first place. I "came out" about having a gay dad through a careful and selective process. Each time I feared I would lose a friend or somehow put my family's privacy or safety at risk. As I grew older, I was less apprehensive about the consequences. I stopped trying to avoid the topic when talking to professors, friends' parents, and coworkers.

Shortly after I graduated from college, I volunteered to lead a support group of teenagers with gay parents. I was curious to meet them, but I wondered if I had anything to offer. At that time I had believed that with rapid changes in attitudes toward homosexuality, these teenagers would see little in my life history that would resonate with theirs.

I was wrong. They were facing the same issues that I had faced in junior high and high school. They wanted to learn from one another about how to tell friends, survive in school, and deal with tension between family members. They wanted to understand the ongoing conflict of loving their parents, yet not feeling safe to be fully open about their families. Even though I differed from those teens by several years and in family composition, our common ground was greater than our differences. After meeting that group, I realized that the sharing of my own family experience had just begun.

WHY THIS BOOK

After choosing to become an advocate for LGBT families, I soon learned that my experience was more common than I had ever imagined. I am part of a population—children of LGBT parents—that is quickly becoming more visible. There are no exact numbers on how many kids in the United States have LGBT parents, but in the past two decades estimates have ranged from one to sixteen million. The numbers on the lower end of the range—one to three million—have been commonly cited by researchers and LGBT family organizers in recent years.[1]

The 2000 U.S. Census reported nearly 600,000 same-sex couples residing in 99.3 percent of the counties across the country. It is highly likely that these statistics are well below the actual numbers of same-sex partners. The obstacle to more accurate numbers is that some people do not feel safe declaring on a government form that they are in a same-sex relationship—especially if they live in a state where it is legal to fire someone for being gay. Of the same-sex households who responded to the census, one-fifth of the male couples and one-third of the female couples are raising children under the age of 18.[2] It's also important to remember that census statistics on same-sex parents reflect only a portion of LGBT families in the U.S. The Census collected data about cohabitation for same-sex couples; it did not collect any data about sexual orientation or transgender identity. These statistics overlook single gay parents, bisexual parents who are partners with someone of the opposite sex, transgender parents, and LGBT people in heterosexual marriages.

As recently as fifteen or twenty years ago, the option to have children seemed out of the question for many people who were coming out. The assumption was that gay people could not have children unless they pretended to be heterosexual by marrying someone of the opposite sex. More single and partnered LGBT people began to challenge that assumption, actively seeking ways to become parents. The impact has snowballed into something significant enough to now be called a "gayby boom." With the increased visibility of LGBT people adding children to their families through adoption, fostering, insemination, and surrogacy, they have been able to share resources and offer peer support to others who also want to parent. No longer are prospective parents left to navigate the path to parenthood alone.

While there are many books about LGBT families, most focus on *becoming* a parent and are written by authors who are gay and lesbian parents themselves. The focus tends to be on the pressing logistics such as telling the grandparents-to-be, choosing a known or unknown sperm donor, or picking a last name with or without a hyphen. There has been very little written about what happens after kids come on the scene.

Over the years I have participated in ongoing discussions about how or if LGBT parents and their children learn to gloss over the challenges our families face in an attempt to gain acceptance by the "mainstream." Many of those challenges have nothing to do with the parents' sexuality, but rather with the complexities of family dynamics that could occur in *any* family. However, since sexual orientation is the issue that puts our families under scrutiny in the first place, it's nearly impossible to acknowledge those other complexities without risking exploitation by opponents to gay parenting. Our families currently lack the "luxury" to be as openly complicated, confusing, or dysfunctional as straight families.

HOW TO USE THIS BOOK

Throughout this book I make several references to people participating on "panels." When LGBT families gather, a programming favorite is the "teen panel," or "young adult panel," for which I have frequently been a moderator. At these presentations, kids of LGBT parents talk about their families to an audience of parents who are given the opportunity to ask questions. *Families Like Mine* is a compilation of the major themes that emerge at nearly every panel: coming out, divorce, school, extended family, AIDS, and the children's sexual orientation. Think of this book as a souped-up panel in print.

Chapter One, "Children of LGBT Parents," explores how kids are affected by the knowledge that people care so much about how they turn out. This sense of being in a fishbowl has as much to do with how these children "turn out" as does the sexual orientation of their parents. Chapter Two, "Coming Out," addresses many of the concerns that parents have about coming out to children. It is mainly for parents who are leaving a marriage, but even same-sex couples who think the situation is obvious to their children will find out why coming out—as an ongoing process—is necessary for all queer families.

Chapter Three, "Family Change," looks at co-parent relationships through the eyes of the children after breakups of both same-sex and opposite-sex couples. If a parent is leaving a marriage or a same-sex partnership, the needs of their children are the same in many ways, but there are also some important differences. I begin the chapter specifically addressing parents who are married and come out to their spouse and children. Following that is information specific to same-sex breakups—a process that can leave children vulnerable to heterosexist loopholes in the legal system. The end of Chapter Three covers issues that both types of families share: co-parenting with an ex and getting back into dating.

Chapter Four, "Out into the World," shows how children navigate homophobia when their parents are not there to help them through it. Chapter Five, "Family-Defining Moments," is about queer families seeking the validation that heterosexual families receive every day.

Chapter Six, "Silent Panic," addresses the impact of AIDS on gay families, a subject that urgently needs to be addressed as national statistics show that new cases have been on the rise among gay men since 1999. Some of the people interviewed in Chapter Six responded to my query specifically because I named HIV/AIDS as a topic this book would cover. Grown children of HIV-positive parents are passionate about telling their stories to help decrease the isolation and stigma that still exists for children in these families today.

Chapters Seven and Eight are in-depth examinations of the hot-button topic of the sexual orientation of sons and daughters. Chapter Seven, "Second Generation" is about the issues queer kids of LGBT parents face—including stigma from their own community. Chapter Eight, "Tourists at Home," is about what happens when heterosexual children grow up to identify as "culturally queer."

This book is not a "how-to" guide. LGBT families are so diverse, it would be impossible to say there is a single "right" way to raise these children. The variety of family composition and experiences also means that not all parts of the book will be applicable to every family. The chapter on AIDS is specific to male parents, for example, and the section on heterosexual divorce will obviously not apply to a parent who has never been married. Readers might still find insight in stories that are notably different from theirs, but if not, it is fine to skip past the information not applicable to a particular family.

Since the launch of my website, I have been contacted regularly not only by LGBT families, but also by service providers—especially teachers, therapists, and clergy. I also receive e-mails from grandparents, aunts and uncles, neighbors, coaches, and friends. I am heartened that they all want to find out how they can best support children they know who have LGBT parents. This book will help these essential allies gain a deeper understanding of the unique needs and challenges of these families.

I also anticipate that adult and teenage sons and daughters will read *Families Like Mine*. They commonly tell me that they would like to talk to their parents about these issues but they do not know how to start the conversation. Let this book be the spark. I hope the variety of voices I compiled for the book will give families permission to honestly acknowledge all of their experiences, not just the moments suitable for photo albums.

About the Participants

This book includes the voices of more than fifty children of LGBT parents, now in their twenties and thirties. I chose to interview grown children rather than teenagers because the safety of time and space from their upbringing means that they have offered responses for this book that are true *for them*. I know that after becoming an adult and moving out on my own, I felt freer to talk about my life experience as *my own* rather than a reflection on whether my parents were *bad* or *good*. I have heard similar sentiments from many of the hundreds of adult sons and daughters I have met over the years. Their stories are based on how they alone observed and interpreted situations when they were younger. I did not contact any of the subjects' parents to double-check the veracity of the facts or their interpretation of them. Their memories might differ from their parents' recollections of a particular incident, but it is the meaning attached to their memories that matters most.

Several times during interviews, participants started to answer a question and then interrupted themselves by saying something like, "This is not what parents like to hear. . . ." They have learned which of their opinions parents love to hear, and which are likely to make LGBT parents feel uncomfortable. But now, as adults, the parent-child power dynamic is better balanced, and the grown children are more willing to talk about all facets of their experience, including parts that could be met with resistance.

Many of the participants come from three cities where there are strong networks for LGBT communities: San Francisco, New York, and Minneapolis. Other participants live in a variety of places, such as Washington, D.C., Hawaii, Florida, Mississippi, and Texas. Some of them I have known for several years; others responded to my request for participants that was passed on through my e-newsletter, LGBT and progressive listserves, and word of mouth.

They come from all kinds of family structures that might be labeled "nontraditional" or "alternative." Because of the ages of these grown children, most of them were born into a heterosexual marriage with one or both parents later coming out. As more LGBT people become parents *after* coming out, there will be more grown children from LGBT families who were adopted, or conceived via insemination or surrogacy.

Several of the children interviewed have younger siblings—often with an age difference of a decade or more. These siblings were added to their family after a formerly married parent re-partnered. In the future, their younger siblings and their peers will provide additional perspectives to the conversations begun by the children who came from heterosexual divorces. Regardless of how their families were formed, the children still face common challenges in a society that questions the validity of their families. Many parents of the gayby boom are surprised to discover that despite growing acceptance these challenges still exist for their children.

For the most part, the people who were willing to be interviewed for this book are comfortable with their family history. They are individuals who, for a variety of reasons, have a desire to be heard. Some feel a connection to other people in similar families and want to be a part of the community. Some are participating out of a sense of duty—they see it as a way to "give back." Others want to talk because they say it's the first time anyone has asked.

Each participant in this book had a choice about using his or her real name or a pseudonym. Those who chose pseudonyms did so for a variety of reasons. Some do not feel that their parents would approve of their being so public with private family information. Some who felt scrutinized as children for having LGBT parents do not want that kind of attention to follow them into their adult life. Others fear that publicly identifying a parent as gay would threaten the parent's job security.

As for the people who chose to use their real names, some requested that I refer to them only by first name to maintain their parents' privacy. Others were fine with using their full name. To some, it was very important that I include their last name; they want to be recognizable to friends and family. Additionally, several of them have previously participated in academic studies on gay parenting in which, as a matter of protocol, researchers made them anonymous. Here, they are named and credited for the insights they share.

AN EXPLANATION OF VOCABULARY

There are many words in this book that might be common to some readers and completely new to others, so I need to explain a few up front.

While some people find the word "queer" to be helpful and affirm-ing, other people are offended by it. I use the word freely in this book in ways that I would not have just a few years ago. It was a shameful and forbidden word in my home growing up, so hearing it used to trig-ger a physical reaction for me, like getting kicked in the gut. More re-cently, I have grown comfortable saying "queer" as I hear it used by activists whom I respect. For my parents' generation, however, the word still evokes its history as a hurtful slur. So while I frequently say "queer," I understand that not everyone cares to reclaim it.

Sons and daughters are often inconsistent when they choose kin-ship terms to refer to their parents' partners. Without a universally un-derstood name for that relationship, children will say "other mother," "stepmother" or simply call her by her first name. In reference to the couple, a child might say "my mom and her partner," "my moms," and "my parents" all in the same conversation. These terms need to be un-derstood within their context. If, for example, a son of a lesbian is talking about his "mom and stepmom," he is referring to his mother's partner, not his father's wife.

Children of LGBT parents are challenged to find concise and in-clusive ways to refer to themselves as a group. One way is to refer to someone as a "colager," which derives from COLAGE—Children of Lesbians and Gays Everywhere. This means that someone has or had one or more parents who are LGBT. It does not necessarily mean that someone is a member of the organization, but since COLAGE built the early foundation for the kids-of-queers community, its name be-came part of the lingo that stuck. Another term, "queerspawn," was coined by Stefan Lynch, the first director of COLAGE. "Queerspawn" has been considered a more radical term, and while some children find it offensive, some people in this book use the term proudly.

Because the word "homophobia" has its limitations for describing all levels of prejudice that LGBT communities face, I add two terms to define the severity of homophobia more comprehensively. At one end of the spectrum of homophobia are people I call "homo-hostile" and at the other end are people I refer to as "homo-hesitant." While a phobia— *fear*—may be at the root of all prejudice, I make a distinction between the people who are intentionally hateful and those who are simply un-certain.

Many readers will already have an idea about what this book should say before they read a word of it. Some LGBT-family supporters will want this to provide evidence that gay parents are perfect, or at least "as good as" straight parents. Some homo-hostile people will carefully comb through the chapters hoping to find documentation of the tragedies children with queer parents have suffered. My intent is not to satisfy either of those assumptions, but rather to advocate for our families to be just that: families.

Fighting for the right for LGBT families to be acknowledged as valid families is a struggle that should not even exist. Someday our so-ciety will find it incomprehensible that queer families were ever con-sidered controversial or that their validity was once debatable. It is with hope for that future that I wrote this book.

One
Children of LGBT Parents: Growing Up Under Scrutiny

It's hard to grow up under a microscope. As kids, we are expected to talk about very adult issues—sex, civil rights, legal and political issues. What other situations are there where people talk to kids and then legislate from there?
—JESSE GILBERT, 30

Many times throughout my life people have been shocked when they find out my father is gay. "I had no idea," they say. "You'd never know just by looking at you." They make me feel like a rare species as their eyes scan me for any abnormalities they missed that could have tipped them off. *Ladies and Gentleman, step right up! Look closely at the child of a gay dad. No horns! No tail! In fact, she could pass for anybody's child.*

What do people *think* kids of LGBT parents "look" like? If they don't know any personally, they might believe the anti-gay rhetoric about why children shouldn't be raised by gay parents: it's abnormal, it's deviant; the children will grow up confused, lacking values and morals; the children will be recruited into homosexuality. This rhetoric is what stands in the way of LGBT parents gaining parental rights equal to those of straight parents.

Every time religious leaders, conservative politicians, or even radio talk-show hosts express their homo-hostile opinions, children in these families cannot help but notice. In 2003, the Vatican released a document opposing gay marriage which stated: "allowing children to be adopted by persons living in such unions would actually mean doing violence to these children." This cruel allegation completely ignored the fact that there are children who are already in these families. These children were being told by a major world religion that being raised by their parents was "not conducive to their full human development."[3]

This Vatican statement is a recent and highly visible example of the homo-hostile rhetoric to which children of LGBT parents are subjected every day. When I was a child, I did not know other people who had gay parents, so when I consistently overheard homo-hostile opinions about gay people's kids being really messed up, even I wondered if it was true. I considered my brother and me to be fortunate for beating the odds and being raised by a *normal* gay dad, not like all those other gay parents who are detrimental to their children's well-being.

Pervasive homo-hostile views are effectively countered by the increased visibility of LGBT families who are gradually shifting social attitudes about gay rights, same-sex marriage, and gay parenting. In March 2002, Rosie O'Donnell officially declared that she is gay in a television interview with Diane Sawyer on *Primetime Thursday*. Rosie's interview called attention to a law in Florida that bans gay people from adopting children. "I don't think America knows what a gay parent looks like," O'Donnell said. "I am the gay parent." The program, which also featured interviews with children adopted and fostered by gay parents, reached 14.4 million households.[4] Hardworking LGBT nonprofit organizations can only dream about having that kind of far-reaching impact in one night.

Bringing LGBT parents and their children into the public eye is necessary for there to be mainstream awareness of LGBT families. These real families show the public that concerns about children raised in LGBT families are based on prejudice and homophobia.

Florida's gay-parent adoption ban passed in 1977, but before the *Primetime* special aired, most people who attended my lectures were shocked to learn the law existed. Now when I refer to the law, more people in the audiences nod in recognition; introducing the personal impact of a public issue is what has made the difference.

With conservative voices adamantly arguing that children are damaged by having parents who are gay, it is not surprising that more reasonable voices in the gay-parenting debate strive to demonstrate how "normal" these families are. At the same time, however, children with LGBT parents who see how they are represented publicly begin to internalize a paradox: to be accepted for being different, they first have to prove that they are "just like" everyone else. LGBT parents need to consider how this public discourse—both positive and negative—affects their children. Inevitably their children consume the same media, which in turn shapes how these kids think and feel about their own families.

In the past few years several professional organizations have released statements of support for the rights of gay parents and their children. Among these organizations are the American Academy of Pediatrics, the American Psychoanalytic Association, the American Academy of Family Physicians, and the American Bar Association. Each statement makes a positive step toward acceptance for LGBT family rights, but they also reinforce to children how vulnerable their families currently are. The right for LGBT families to exist is the subject of debate, and children begin to figure out that the outcome of this debate rests on how they "turn out."

One teen remembers being approached by a local TV station that wanted to interview her about "what it was like to grow up in a lesbian household." She laughed at the notion of her life being presented like an exposé. She ate cereal in the morning, went to school, studied music, did homework, and hung out with friends. "What is it," she wondered out loud, "that they think they will find in a lesbian household?"

Even a well-meaning reporter who asks an eight-year-old, "What is it like having two moms?" suggests to the child that she *should* have a formed opinion about her family—something that other kids her age are not expected to do. When so many people are determined to find out what it is like to grow up in these families, a major part of the growing-up experience is the realization that how you turn out matters to more than just your own parents.

DESIRABLE(?) OUTCOMES

There is a lot at stake around the debates about how children fare in families with LGBT parents. Evidence showing that children in queer families are well adjusted offers queer families hope that they might gain better access to the civil and legal rights available to straight-parent families. Evidence implying that children are not well adjusted adds fuel to the argument that only heterosexual parents should raise children. Adding to the complications of these debates is that even supporters and opponents of gay parenting disagree on what outcomes determine if a child is "well adjusted."

Almost any article about gay parenting will vaguely reference "research" or "studies" about how the children "turn out." Such media reports cover the "pro" side of the debate by stating that research indicates that children of gay parents are no different from children with straight parents. The results of academic studies, however, are simplified by the media for mainstream audiences and herein lies the problem. When science is watered down for popular consumption, generalities are made and subtlety is lost.

The historical context for the early studies offers insight into the political climate for LGBT parenting, and why the research has been so important for these families. The studies in the 1980s focused mainly on children of lesbian mothers—once automatically assumed "unfit"—to "prove" that such children could still meet certain criteria of what would be considered acceptable developmental norms for children. Those norms, however, were defined within homophobic parameters.

To ensure that gay parents would not be denied custody when seeking a divorce after coming out, the research needed to demonstrate that a gay parent would not adversely affect a child's development. The findings needed to counter homophobic fears, namely that the children would be no more likely to be gay themselves. And since so much of homophobia is based on notions of gender nonconformity, daughters turning out to be less feminine and sons turning out to be less masculine would also be cause for concern. Research introduced in custody cases assured the court that children of gay parents demonstrated no significant differences from children of straight parents. The assumptions have been that it would be somehow bad if children were more flexible in their gender-based behavior, and that children coming out as gay would be an undesirable outcome.

A more progressive perspective was introduced in an article in the April 2001 issue of the *American Sociological Review*. Judith Stacey and Timothy J. Biblarz, both sociology professors at the University of Southern California, re-examined the data of studies from 1981–1998 on children of lesbian and gay parents. Eighteen of the twenty-one studies were on children of lesbian mothers; three were on children of gay fathers. Stacey and Biblarz concluded that contrary to previous conclusions, children in these studies demonstrated some differences from their counterparts who have straight parents.[5] The article was controversial because it challenged a core idea that LGBT communities have been eager to promote: that we're just like everyone else—"everyone else" being families with straight parents.

The authors' interpretation of the data suggested that the tendency of children with gay parents to challenge traditional ideas of gender roles and sexuality was higher than that of children with het-

erosexual parents. Among the findings, more of the research participants with gay and lesbian parents expressed an interest in careers outside of gender assumptions (female astronauts, for example) than did
those with straight parents.

Children in these studies were also *more open to the idea* of being in
a same-sex relationship.[6] Homo-hostile people typically interpret this
particular finding as an indicator of homosexual identity. To the children, however, not rejecting the possibility of ever being attracted to
someone of the same sex simply means they are less homophobic than
most people who identify as heterosexual. In a casual conversation
about how this nuance is lost on people who are homophobic, one
straight daughter summed it up by saying, "They assume our lack of
fear equals queer."

While homo-hostile people often consider the differences described in the Stacey/Biblarz article as being undesirable outcomes,
Stacey disagrees, which is partly why she was interested in this research. "Almost all of the studies," Stacey says, "have either evaded
those issues [gender and sexuality], or claimed that there are no differences. . . . I felt that that was an untenable position, and it was also
homophobic, because it implied that there would be something wrong
with more people turning out to not be exclusively heterosexual."

When the article was published, it attracted a lot of media attention. Some LGBT parents felt threatened by the ideas it presented and
worried about reactions from the right wing. Predictably, homo-hostile
organizations pointed to the article as evidence that gay parents really
do have a negative impact on their children. There were other LGBT
parents, however, who saw the new analysis as reason for recognizing
and celebrating their differences instead of fearing them.

Lisa Bennett, deputy director for Human Rights Campaign's FamilyNet says that regardless of the interpretations of social science research, it is not fair for LGBT people to have to rely on studies on
their children in order for parents to be granted rights that are auto-

matic for other parents. "The issues of equal rights should rest on principle, not on research," Bennett says. "There is no other population that you can look at and say they have certain rights because the children turned out in X or Y way."

How do the kids of LGBT parents really "turn out"? It depends on the kid. And it depends on who is asking—and why.

THE BURDEN OF LEARNING THE "RIGHT" ANSWERS

Between the debates in the media and overheard conversations, many children in queer families grow up with the sense that their lives are not their own—they are *symbols* of something much bigger. They figure out that they are being observed, and that because of their parents, their otherwise normal lives are interesting or even exotic to outsiders. Tina Fakhrid-Deen, 29, who is heterosexual, says that other people's fascination with children of lesbian and gay parents affected her feelings about herself:

> I'm nowhere near as oppressed as my mom, but I feel I can understand that oppression because we as children of gay parents have been silenced our whole lives, too. We know what it's like, feeling like we are going to hell, or that we are some kind of zoo people. Something to be studied, not loved or embraced or thought of as humans.

Parents wish their children were oblivious to their families being judged, but children cannot help but overhear debates about whether gay people have the "right" to have children, and many of them take it personally. Opposition to their parents' right to have children feels like an attack on their very existence. For some children, defending gay parenthood is defending their right to exist. Some children choose to speak in the media to demystify LGBT families. They have learned that simply being seen as a "regular kid" can melt away prejudice.

Every time children with LGBT parents agree to talk to a journalist, participate in research, or even come out about their family in a social setting, they know they are not only representing their own families—they are opening the window to an entire population that is otherwise invisible. With such intense scrutiny, they are aware of their burden to literally represent millions. Understanding that what they say might influence public policy impedes their freedom to talk openly about their lives. There is an ongoing fear that anything they disclose could be manipulated to discredit their parents, and that any ambivalence or disclosure of difficulties within their home would reflect poorly on their parents, and in turn, would be used to build a case to limit LGBT-family rights.

Jessi Hempel's family was in turmoil when her father came out. Despite her personal experience, she is in support of gay parenting, so she glossed over what had really happened. "I always said [my dad is gay] in a matter-of-fact way, a smiley way," says Jessi, 27, "to let people think that I was totally fine with it and that it was a totally happy process. But I wasn't [totally fine with it] at that point. . . . I struggled with talking about the real experience because that was really hard. . . . I focused on the party line of what people want and need to hear to accept gay parents."

One issue that children commonly defend is gay male parents' choices to raise children without a mother or lesbian mothers' choice to raise children without a father. Out of love for their parents and awareness that their families are being judged by how they respond, children feel the pressure to satisfy everyone's worries by dismissing the notion that they have any interest in a parent of the other gender, even if they have not completely resolved the issue. Jesse Gilbert was raised in a women-centered "urban commune" and did not know his biological father until he was eleven. He explains how the scrutiny affected him:

> When I was younger, I was very aware of the assumption: two women plus a son equals fucked-up guy. You get these very concerned liberal reporters asking, "Didn't you miss your dad? Wasn't that hard?" This is an issue that can't be boiled down to a sound bite. There is a real story to the whole question of my father, but then there was this public persona that I felt I had to present. [My lesbian parents] weren't coming to me and saying, "Don't talk about [your feelings about not knowing your dad]. You have to present yourself to be just fine." It was internal pressure. I felt protective of my family. You are aware of the political issue. You are aware of what you are saying and how they will judge you.

No matter how nicely a researcher or journalist asks if a child would want a dad (in the case of lesbian mothers) or a mother (in the case of gay dads), children still know what is really being asked. The real question is: Should your parents be your parents? Answering with the "right" answer means children have to defend their parents by proving how "normal" they are.

THE PRESSURE TO BE PERFECT:
A DIFFERENT KIND OF CLOSET

When LGBT families are profiled in the media, readers, listeners, and viewers get to find out how "normal" these families are. Most news articles that are going to report on gay parenting in what would be considered a "neutral" position rely on a formula that makes it easier to introduce the idea to readers. It starts out with a profile of a typical child. *Like any five-year-old, Mia is a little nervous about her first day of kindergarten.* The article will mention a quintessential family activity in a gender-neutral way. *Around the dinner table her parents are taking turns telling Mia about all the exciting things she will get to do at school.* Then comes the kicker: *Just the typical all-American family except for one thing—her parents are lesbians.* It's as if by opening with a gender-neutral description, homo-hostile readers will be fooled into hanging on long enough to read about gay families as human beings.

The children in articles and on TV are usually featured as the "other side" to a story on gay parenting where a homo-hostile spokesperson claims that having gay parents is detrimental to children. The popular, successful, and confident children in the story are presented as "proof" to challenge that claim. Nobody is in trouble at school. Nobody throws tantrums or threatens to run away. Nobody is experimenting with drugs. Ever. Did I mention that the kids think their parents are the coolest? Of course any family who volunteers to be in the media wants to present themselves in the best possible light. Unless they are the Osbournes, they prefer to save their bickering for off-camera.

Always presenting this sanitized version of LGBT families in the media, however, feeds broader society—and other LGBT families and their kids—a very limited perspective of how children of LGBT families "should" be. I receive e-mails from sons and daughters whose experiences are as diverse as those in any other family. Some of their families are struggling with depression, alcoholism, or domestic abuse; others are not. Some want nothing to do with anything remotely gay; others love going to Pride. Some are failing classes or getting suspended; others are on the honor roll.

When media stories about gay parenting feature only high-achievers to show how "normal" these kids are, it becomes easy to overlook that not all children of LGBT parents have a circle of supportive friends, are class president, and lettering in three sports. Children with struggles remain invisible to the public eye not only because the families do not want that kind of attention, but because journalists are not eager to feature them. The fear that LGBT parents will be blamed and politically penalized for having less-than-perfect offspring forces these issues underground, isolating kids and families. Being out as an LGBT family but always feeling the pressure to demonstrate that everything is "fine" can feel like leaving one closet for another.

Because of the constant focus on how kids will be affected by growing up in these families, issues surrounding a parent's sexuality become confused with issues that could very well be unrelated. Is a child falling behind in school because both of her parents are women, or is it because she has an undiagnosed learning disability? Is a teen skipping school because of problems with his gay family, or is it just because he hates algebra? Does a gay father assume his daughter's social withdrawal is because of his sexual orientation, or could it be that she is temperamentally shy?

Parents who get so focused on how their sexuality will affect their kids forget to consider children's appropriate developmental states as the reason for a particular behavior. When I spoke to a group of LGBT parents who were all raising preteen children, I made a joke about the looming stage when their children would feel embarrassed by their parents. The parents were not amused. Their children *adore* them right now, and are even bragging to the mail carrier about how cool it is to have two mommies. They can't imagine that there will be a time when this will change—even if it is normal adolescent behavior. For example, when children stop letting their parents kiss them good-bye when they are dropped off at school, LGBT parents might wonder if it is because their children are uncomfortable about their family. More likely it's because the child has hit a stage where it is uncool to be seen kissing parents. That has nothing to do with sexual orientation.

One sixteen-year-old was relieved when she heard about other kids in LGBT families having arguments and getting grounded, because it gave her permission to admit that the same thing happens in her home. Up to that point she didn't even tell her close friends about fights she had in her family because she worried that the truth would reflect poorly on her parents as lesbians.

At twenty-eight, Ari is more comfortable talking openly about his family than he was as a child. Growing up, he kept quiet about his gay father and lesbian mother to try to protect them. Shuttling between two homes after the divorce, Ari did not want his parents' sexuality to be "blamed" for any of their family's issues. He has since discovered that "most families are dysfunctional regardless of sexual orientation," but it was not until he and his older brother were in their midtwenties that they felt comfortable discussing their childhood even with each other. "When we started to ask ourselves questions about our past," Ari says, "of course our parents' sexual orientation was part of what we talked about, because that was part of our experience."

Discerning which social stressors are connected to the parents' sexuality, and which have to do with other issues, is more complicated when parents assume that any conflict is because of "the gay thing." Aidan, 29, grew up with a single teenage mother in Missouri. He feels ambivalent about his relationship with his lesbian mother, but her sexuality is not the reason.

"Growing up, I was never very close with her," says Aidan, "and now I'm not close at all. I believe she thinks it's because of her lifestyle. I have no problem with her lifestyle. If she was married to a man, I still wouldn't be close with her. . . . She is very sweet and loving, but her life is a wreck."

Over the years Aidan's mother has been suicidal, has struggled with drug addiction, and cannot keep a job. Aidan learned to rely on himself at a young age, so "by [the age of] twelve, I was my own person." While his mother—and perhaps judgmental outsiders—assumes his emotional distance is because she is lesbian, Aidan sees that as a separate issue.

Children themselves are not always able to separate their parents' sexual orientation from family problems. After I gave a lecture on a small college campus, one student sent me an e-mail within the hour. Brittany, whose own mother is lesbian, came to hear what I had to say about gay people raising children because she was solidly against it.

"From the time I was about eight or nine until I was seventeen," Brittany wrote, "my mom had a partner who lived with us. Her partner was a drug addict and very abusive to my mom and me and my brother . . . due to this I think that it made me want to cast homosexuality in a bad light."

The abuse at home in combination with not knowing other people with LGBT parents led Brittany to equate LGBT people with terrible parenting. But as she heard about the diverse experiences of other sons and daughters, Brittany began to question her assumption that all children in LGBT households were abused:

> It really wasn't until your lecture that I really have changed my views on homosexuals raising children. [Now] my general feelings are that there is nothing wrong with being homosexual, or with homosexuals having children. It still amazes me— the stories you tell of children who aren't afraid to speak out about it. I don't really have the courage yet to talk about my mom, especially since she doesn't like to talk about it now.

Brittany's story is not one you will hear on a panel, nor would it be highlighted in a sympathetic study about gay parenting. She is not a person who will come forward when a journalist is looking for children to interview. Her family is not a testament to the strengths of LGBT families, but it is her truth.

Acknowledging that in some families children are neglected and abused at the hands of LGBT parents is taboo in many LGBT family circles. The concern is that a few LGBT parents who abuse their children will be used as examples to build a case for why no LGBT people are fit to be parents. Heterosexual parents who abuse their children, however, represent only themselves. The Andrea Yates story is one of countless examples of how differently abusive parenting is treated when it is committed by someone who is heterosexual. The bathtub drowning of her five children evoked a debate about postpartum depression, but the tragedy did not result in other heterosexual parents having to worry about Yates making them "look bad."

FAMILY DIVERSITY AWAY FROM THE SPOTLIGHT

The increased visibility of LGBT families in the public eye means that the general public is learning about LGBT families—but with a limited understanding of the diversity within the community. One of the first images that comes to mind for most people when they think of "gay parenting" is two women raising children through insemination or two men raising children through surrogacy. LGBT families are much more diverse than that, but because these types of families are currently the most controversial, they get a disproportionate amount of coverage in the media.

For example, media coverage might lead the public to believe that the majority of gay dads become parents through surrogacy. Growing Generations, the first surrogacy agency founded specifically for gay men, was founded in 1996 and celebrated their first birth in 1998. By the middle of 2003, the agency had assisted in fewer than two hundred births—a tiny fraction in the big picture of gay-parenting statistics.

Media representation is also disproportionate along lines of class since families created through these biomedical procedures are more likely to represent high socioeconomic levels. For women, getting pregnant through donor insemination can cost anywhere from a few hundred to tens of thousands of dollars, depending on whether a woman needs to pursue fertility treatment. Expenses for gay men creating a child through surrogacy are in the range of $50,000 to $70,000. These expenses are prohibitive for lower-income families who want to raise children, so they are rarely profiled in the media.

Wealthy people also tend to be in a better position to be "out." They might work at a corporation that sees their gay employees as adding to the diversity of the workplace. Or if they are well-off, the idea of losing a job after coming out represents only a temporary setback. For lower-income people, losing their jobs represents a far greater loss, so they are less willing to jeopardize their situations by granting an interview with the media. This is understandable, but it skews public perception of what LGBT families "look like."

Additionally, the lack of LGBT families of color in the public eye creates the perception that there are few such families. This is not true. For example, although LGBT parents who are African-American are not seen frequently in the media, a recent survey of more than 2,500 black LGBT people found that 32 percent of the women and 15 percent of the men had biological children.[7]

"Right now our voices are limited," says Tina, who is African-American and the daughter of a lesbian. "All LGBT families are assumed to be middle-class and white." In her experience, most African-American lesbian mothers keep their sexuality very private and don't care to make it political. They are even less interested in making their children visible. "It's not about activism," Tina explains about the African-American lesbian mothers she knows, "it's about living their lives. When I talk about [families being more visible], a lot of times their reaction is, 'What's it to you?'"

It might also seem like every gay family is from Manhattan or San Francisco, but part of the reason families from those and other cities are featured in the media is that other families can't take the risk. For example, when Mississippi was debating the anti-adoption bill that became law in 2000, a television producer called me in search of families from that state who could represent the pro-gay parenting perspective. He was discouraged that he couldn't find anyone to agree to speak on-camera. It had not occurred to him how potentially dangerous it could be for a gay parent to be identified on a statewide television show when a bill against gay-parent adoption was likely to become law.

Although children of LGBT families who fit certain socioeconomic, racial, and geographic categories receive at least limited representation in the media, children in many other kinds of LGBT families do not see their experience reflected at all. These families include children who have special needs, children raised by queer grandparents, and children with single parents, bisexual parents, and transgender parents. Media representations of LGBT families have yet to catch up to reflect their true diversity.

The Impact of the Public Image on Private Lives

When images of the "right" kind of gay American family are the only images put forth, families that do not meet that standard wonder what is wrong with them and end up feeling more isolated than before. When troubled parents don't seek support, the myth that problems in LGBT families do not exist continues. Children, taking the cue from their parents, hesitate to be open about their everyday lives for fear that it will be misinterpreted.

Just as rhetoric can influence a child's response in public, parents' responses to the rhetoric hinders open communication between parent and child. Most sons and daughters intrinsically understand their mothers' and fathers' desire to be acknowledged as successful parents. This is a reality for both straight and LGBT families. However, this desire is magnified for LGBT families because of societal homophobia. On numerous occasions parents have talked to me in front of their children, saying things like, "Some families are different because of re-

ligious or cultural backgrounds. In our family, the parents aren't heterosexual. Sure, that makes us different, but it's really a nonissue.
We're raising our kids to think for themselves so they won't have problems with this."

Children, who are extremely sensitive to the scrutiny that society
has placed upon their LGBT families, have their own interpretation of
such comments. In their minds they hear: "If you encounter any struggles regarding my sexual orientation, it will be very painful for me. I
will feel like a bad parent. Don't disappoint me." They are put in a
caretaking role to affirm their parents' success as queer parents.

"I'm not comfortable with the poster-child mentality," says Jesse
about the unspoken expectations for how children should talk about
their lives. "If speaking on the topic of gay parents is reduced to a
cheerleader role, where you just have to give them the strength to
carry on, you can never have a real conversation about it."

Jesse says that when LGBT parent groups invite him to speak,
they usually expect his perspective to be completely positive. "They
want me to go up there [in front of the audience] and say, 'Everything
was fine. The rest of the world sucks, but you parents are great.'"

He remembers one time in particular when his candid comments
made parents especially uncomfortable. "I was under the impression
that I had been invited to speak because they actually wanted that
honesty," says Jesse. When the parents grew annoyed that he shared
difficult aspects of his childhood, he says he felt like telling them: "If
you don't like what I'm saying right now, wait until your kids grow up.
You've got a baby boom right now, and they look pretty cute, but wait
until they are in their twenties."

Parents today are often surprised when they find that their children are presenting one reality to their parents but living another.
Children can be so successful at covering up the realities of teasing,
harassment, or their own internalized homophobia that parents are
oblivious to them. I received a phone call one spring from a mother

who learned that her sixth-grade daughter was being taunted by class-mates only after the guidance counselor called home. "And to make things worse," this mother said, "I find out that this has been going on since the beginning of the school year! I had no reason to think any-thing was wrong. Why didn't she tell me earlier?"

Another lesbian mother said her daughter had been enthusiastic about transferring to another high school. It wasn't until after the fact that she felt comfortable telling her mom that the main reason she wanted to leave her previous school was to escape the homophobic climate. Until then, this mother had no idea what her daughter had been hiding from her.

Many sons and daughters share similar stories of times when they felt they had to protect their parents from their real experiences for fear that they would seem unsupportive. Aaron, 28, continues to be bothered by homophobic jokes and is conflicted about how to respond when he hears them. He has never talked to his mom and her partner about it because "there's not a lot they can do about it," he says. "They're gay. That's fine. But if I bust out with how I feel about it, it's raising a problem without offering a good solution. I'm not going to ask them to stop being gay. And I'm not going to ask them to stop being out about it."

Aaron doesn't want his discomfort with homophobia to be misun-derstood as discomfort about his family. To him, talking about it would frame his parents' sexuality—rather than the homophobic comments—as the real problem.

Thomas Fronczak, a therapist in Providence, and founder of the Gay Fathers of Rhode Island Support Network, says that children's re-sistance to talking about homophobia with their parents is to be ex-pected. "In the normal course of development," Fronczak says, "children often protect the honor and integrity of their families. Chil-dren with LGBT parents . . . have been known to take strong stances to protect their parents from painful homophobic rhetoric."

Jessi has observed the phenomenon both as the daughter of a gay father and as a COLAGE volunteer, working closely with younger children in these families:

> There's a sense that children have to account for their parents and protect them. I don't like that. You have to become one-dimensional in public when you are the child of a queer parent. They always have kind things to say about their parents and that's not the truth. Kids of queer parents are real people. And real people, especially adolescents, sometimes don't like their parents. It doesn't always have to do with being gay.

As a child and teen, I, too, thought that being extra careful about how I talked about my family was part of my job as a supportive daughter. What was different for me, however, was that public discussion about gay parenting was rare in the 1980s. I felt a responsibility to present my family as "normal," but at least that burden was not connected to a larger political landscape as LGBT parenting rights are today. Children need permission to share their real feelings with their parents rather than thinking they should tell their parents what they want to hear. Parents can remind their children that it is not their "job" to defend them.

LOOKING BACK: GROWING UP OUTSIDE THE NORM

When sons and daughters are adults, they can look back on their childhood with the more comprehensive perspectives that come with distance and maturity. Grown children who have the freedom to reflect on their families without having to defend or downplay their influence often talk about "going against the grain." While it can some-times be difficult not to be part of the in-crowd at various stages of childhood, many sons and daughters say they are fortunate to have been raised outside the norm.

The fear of raising children in an environment that is different from their peers' is that they will grow up to be confused. But what might be considered confusing to some feels liberating to others. Ac-cepting that there is more than one way to do something encourages children to question rigid societal expectations and explore what makes them personally happy. When these children grow up, most are proud of how their upbringing made them different. David Wells, 28, says that having a gay dad encouraged him to think differently about gender in ways that most straight men do not. "[Having personal con-nections to gay men] has opened my mind as an adult to allow me to drop my masculinity sometimes," David says. "I can be more effemi-nate and openly affectionate with other men and not have to feel in-secure or weird about it."

From the outside looking in, homophobic people might see David's ease in crossing boundaries of gender behavior as evidence that he is "confused." If his dad had been straight, this line of thinking goes, David would have a clearer sense of how to be a "real man."

Similarly, Leslie "Les" Addison, 35, who is lesbian, attributes her expanding view of womanhood to her upbringing:

> I think that because my mother was in a lesbian relationship during most of my childhood, she felt a higher level of pres-sure to be a "perfect" parent and to have me conform to soci-etal gender norms. At the same time, because I lived in a house full of women, I saw women taking on various roles and responsibilities—running a business, mowing the lawn, cook-ing dinner, paying bills, etc. I saw women as having unlimited potential.

David and Les's perspectives dismiss typical ideas of how men and women are supposed to behave. To people who are homo-hostile, these attitudes could be considered undesirable—threats to American "family values." Socially conservative people consider it a "failure" when adult children do not conform to traditional roles or do not create traditional families. The children themselves, however, appreciate these differences.

Coming from a gay family in a predominately heterosexual society meant that the world I knew best was constantly being challenged. My parents taught me to believe that despite society's homophobia, my family was a good family. They helped me understand that the negative assumptions I heard about homosexuality did not have to be part of my own truth. Discovering that my otherwise unremarkable family was by societal standards abhorrent made me suspicious of values that the mainstream touted as ideal. I learned that I needed to critically analyze any assumption that broader society presented to me in absolute terms. Phrases like "because that's just how it is" or "because that's how it's done" have never satisfied me. They only provoked me to ask more questions.

Filtering through societal assumptions and pressures was a skill I developed for enduring prejudice against my family. After I began to doubt the validity of homophobia and my world didn't implode, it was easier for me to challenge other cultural expectations. While classmates in junior high were paging through fashion magazines to keep up with the trends, I wondered why women put so much energy into presenting themselves in the ways magazines said they should. The bodies and faces of these models were flawless. How could I possibly meet these standards? Then it occurred to me that I didn't have to. Similar to how I knew I did not have to internalize societal homophobia, I also did not have to internalize societal messages about how women needed to look to be valued. Just as no church, or law, or bully was going to dictate how I felt about my family, no magazine, or model, or fad was going to dictate how I felt about my body.

Many adult children share this confidence in questioning society because of what they have learned in their families. Monica Canfield-Lenfest, 22, was seventeen when her father came out as transgender:

> With gender, we are taught that a dad is a man and a mother is a woman. And when the gender role and the parent's role don't line up, it's a really intense thing. It's kind of like I shouldn't exist. And if society is telling me that I shouldn't exist, then what *can* I believe? I think that for me, a big thing I have learned from all of this is the ability and necessity to be a social critic—to automatically question society.

Monica's words echo those of other children who are grateful that they have learned to challenge conventional assumptions. Heather, 26, says that having a transgender father has helped her "become a better person." "I think," says Heather, "that with every experience that makes you examine your own values and what you thought was your own reality, you derive a lot of strength from those tests. . . . It's like a muscle that breaks down, but it builds back stronger."

Being in families that challenged societal norms often means that children in LGBT families grow up to be more open-minded and more empathetic toward people who are different from them. Adult children can look back and appreciate the gifts they gained from being part of a family that was different. Unfortunately, the idea that having LGBT parents "builds character" is of little consolation to someone in the middle of adolescence.

Noel Black, 30, is a "bothie," meaning he had a lesbian mom and a gay dad. Growing up in Colorado Springs, he had two friends who had lesbian mothers, but he was the only one who had a gay father as well. When he was sixteen he found out his father had AIDS.

"I felt I had been stricken with an added curse," says Noel, "although I realize now that I was also prone to a fairly brooding and introspective outlook regardless. . . . Looking back, it's hard to relate to the pensive and questioning kid I was . . . [I] am pretty much over it other than feeling that having the experience has, happily, made me the rather normal freak I am."

Over the years he has stayed in contact with both of these friends from childhood, but neither of them was interested in being involved in LGBT family activities. Noel says his friends are people "like many of the millions of kids with some queer parent or another who realize that in the bigger picture, everyone faces the freakishness of life in their own ways."

Knowing that the possibilities are much more numerous than what is traditionally emphasized can make it difficult to fit into the predominantly straight culture—a culture that relies on its rigid notions of gender, class, race, and sexuality. While these children appreciate having a broader perspective about gender—men who can be sensitive and women who can be more assertive—some ask themselves if life would be "easier" if they could feel satisfied in the traditional roles they are expected to play.

Joe Hake, 22, thinks that having a lesbian mother meant he developed "female tendencies," making him different from the typical straight guy. "I have a hard time meeting women that are really my type," Joe says. "If I'm talking to a girl who wants to do the traditional woman thing, that's like major points against her right off the bat. . . . Sometimes I do wonder if women are more attracted to steak-and-potatoes *Monday Night Football* guys who are going to treat them like crap."

For Jenny Laden, 32, having a gay dad influenced how she thinks about expectations in partnerships, and finds these expectations to be incompatible with those of most heterosexual men. She does not want to be married unless she finds a partner "who is truly my equal. I'd like a partner who can add to my life, not drain my energy." Nevertheless, she wonders what her life would be like if she were content to live out traditional expectations.

"I'm constantly at odds with the American ideal," Jenny explains, "because it looks like a nice little picture: the husband, the kids, the house. It's easy for me to reduce it to this romantic notion." Despite this fantasy of fitting in, living her life outside the norm has been freeing for Jenny. "For me, there's not a set script of how my life is supposed to happen. The possibilities are much greater."

Soon after I graduated from college, I did my first media interview. I told the journalist that although I was seeing attitudes toward gay families change for the better, there was still a long way to go. Surprised by this comment, she said, "But gay families have made it onto the front page of the newspaper. Aren't you pleased to see such success?"

Being profiled in the paper simply because I was from *one of those* families is *progress*, but it is not success. Success will be when a child with LGBT parents can be profiled for *some other reason* and the mention of his or her family can be referenced without sexual orientation becoming the main focus. Success will be when the point of profiling a child of LGBT parents is to celebrate his or her accomplishments, not to serve as proof of anything regarding queer families.

Until LGBT parenting rights are equivalent to those of straight parents, the public will continue to scrutinize the lives of children of LGBT parents. It's unfortunate that it is necessary to counter the claims that these children are negatively affected by their parents' sexuality. Parents need to be sensitive to how that scrutiny may be affecting their children's perceptions of themselves. By celebrating differences rather than denying them, parents demonstrate to their children that they should not have to be "just like" straight families in order to gain equal rights.

It is unfair to expect children to prove how smart, cute, ambitious, precocious, or "normal" they are in order for their family to be deemed worthy of social acceptance. LGBT families should be allowed to be just as wacky, troubled, or complex as any other American family. It is the truth of our humanity—not the myth of "perfect" conformity—that will one day help LGBT families celebrate full equality.

Two

Coming Out:
A Family Process

When Dad came out, it changed how I related to her. I think a large part of it was that my dad didn't have to pretend anymore and she could just be herself.

—MONICA CANFIELD-LENFEST, 22

Coming out of the closet—that is, openly declaring one's sexual orientation or gender identity—is a major concern for parents. Their questions are many: *How should I talk to my kids about it? When is it too early? Is it ever too late? What if I say the wrong thing?*

There is no single way to come out to children, nor is there a perfect time. Coming-out stories cover a wide spectrum, from the anticlimactic to the heartbreaking. Regardless of the circumstances or reactions, children experience tension, distancing, and confusion when their parents don't talk about it—even when the situation seems obvious.

When my father moved out of the house in 1978, he told my eight-year-old brother that he was gay. Mom and Dad decided that since I was only five, I was too young to understand what it meant to be gay, and they would tell me when I was older. Dad explained to Ben that he had special feelings for his friend Russ, but that not everyone would approve of these feelings. My father wrote down what he had said so that Ben could refer back to it if he wanted to, and as a reminder that he could talk to Dad about it whenever he wanted.

My brother was uncomfortable keeping this secret from his only sibling. Wasn't I going to wonder why Dad's "roommate" seemed to go everywhere with us? Ben repeatedly asked my mother, "Did you tell her yet?" But my mother kept telling him to wait.

Dad had told Ben that he might hear words like "faggot" and "queer" but that these words were hurtful and shouldn't be said. ("Queer" had yet to be reclaimed by LGBT people as it has been in recent years.) One day while riding in the car with my mom and Ben, I innocently described something as being queer.

"Mom," my brother said, "Abby said 'queer'!" My mother was not prepared for this conversation, but she said, "We don't use that word in our family. It's a not-nice word for someone who is gay." She waited another moment and then asked, "Abby, do you know what 'gay' means?"

"Yes," I said. "It's when two women or two men love each other. Like Dad and Russ are gay."

Trying not to reveal her surprise at my response, Mom calmly told me which of their friends knew why Dad had moved out of the house. I learned that because "some people think it's terrible to be gay," we would have to be careful about whom we told. From that moment on, I began a lifetime of seeking out allies and avoiding people I perceived as homophobic and therefore threats to my family.

The conversation I had with my mother is the closest I can get to how I found out my dad was gay. I don't remember any previous conversations about the topic. My experience would have been a lot different—and more negative—if my parents had indeed waited until they thought I was old enough to understand what "gay" meant. By that time, I easily could have adopted some of the homophobic attitudes that are prevalent in our society. If that had happened, I would have had to "come to terms" with my dad being gay rather than simply integrating it into my life along with all the other information I was absorbing as a young child.

In some families, coming out is a revelation that explodes into a messy argument. In others, LGBT parents wonder why they were so worried to begin with; their children react with little more than a shrug. For some children, the news takes a while to sink in. For other children, it can be a relief—a missing piece that helps answer other questions.

Amber Love, 25, noticed that her mother was harboring a secret that was causing her stress. Her mother told her she was worried Amber wouldn't love her after the truth was revealed. Amber could not imagine what the big secret was, but thought perhaps it had something to do with her mother's activism during the Vietnam War:

> I became convinced she had helped bomb something and we were going to be fleeing to Brazil in the very near future. But Mom's most radical protest was running an underground newspaper. Her secret was coming out of the closet. Only because I recognized my mother's extreme distress did I refrain from saying something to the effect of "Well, it's about damn time," or "No shit, Sherlock!" I had just turned sixteen and I had known for years.

Coming out to children can be scary and awkward and unpredictable. The harsher memories of the experience fade with time, letting parents gloss over their worries of rejection and their struggle to figure out what to say. Years later, what was once an all-consuming issue is often remembered and retold as a smoother event than it actually was: "And then I came out to my kids." Such oversimplifications make the already momentous task of coming out feel all the more impossible to parents who are about to tell their children. ("Other parents make it sound so easy. Why does it feel so difficult for me?")

Countless LGBT parents have taken the risk, and their families have worked through it.

Kids don't always react in ways their parents had hoped. Adam, 25, was twelve when he learned his mother was lesbian. He said that his initial reaction was one of disgust and anger:

> I just couldn't understand how this could happen. I mean, we are taught that men and women fall in love and get married, not two women or two men; [I thought] *those* people are weird. I think that they should have told us a long time before I was in adolescence. Perhaps if my sister and I were about seven or eight, that would have been a good time, since at that age society's negativity toward homosexuality hasn't crept into the child's head yet.

Homophobia, like other forms of prejudice, is taught. Adam already had this prejudice in his mind before his mom came out. For me, knowing at such a young age that my dad was gay had a major influence on how I felt about him as a gay man, and how I felt about homosexuality in general. When I overheard a debate on TV about homosexuality or a news report about a gay rights demonstration, the idea that people were speaking out against gay people made no sense. The images of homosexuality presented by the opposition were so negative: deviant people who were going to hell; perverts who were corrupting children. My dad was gay, and so were many of his friends. None of them fit the descriptions of the evil homosexual. What, I wondered, did these grown-ups see that I did not?

Even though I seemed fine about my dad being gay, my family would have many conversations about it over the years. As I matured, I had different questions about my father's sexuality. There were stages in my life when I didn't feel comfortable asking them, but it was reassuring to know that I could when I wanted to.

WHY COME OUT?

While the reasons for coming out may be obvious to some parents, to others—especially those who are not geographically close to strong LGBT communities—those reasons are less clear. Understanding the importance of coming out at all is the first step in preparing to come out to children.

The homo-hostile perspective claims that coming out—and being out—is inappropriate. Why, they argue, should anyone go around announcing who they want to have sex with? LGBT people should just keep their sexuality to themselves.

The queer-supportive view is that coming out is necessary for both personal and community integrity. When LGBT people do not come out, they remain in isolation. Isolation creates a myth that LGBT people are freaks of nature who exist "somewhere else." Maintaining this myth cultivates one of the most powerful weapons used against the LGBT community: shame. Shame, in turn, is used to justify the limitation of rights and dignity for LGBT people.

In addition to the importance of being visible, coming out is necessary because sexuality is a core part of our identity as human beings. Whether or not people are sexually active, they still have a sexual identity. And in some cases, even a person's sexual behavior does not reflect a person's actual sexual orientation, as demonstrated by men and women who marry people of the opposite sex as a way to hide or deny that they are gay.

The anti-gay argument against coming out ignores a blatant double standard. Heterosexuals announce their sexuality in countless ways every day; a quick kiss in public between a mom and a dad earns approving smiles from onlookers, as if strangers are thinking, "How sweet that the romance is still there, and that their children are growing up in a loving household." Switching the gender of one of these parents brings totally different reactions. A quick kiss in public between two moms or two dads can warrant awkwardness and furrowed brows from homophobic onlookers. Instead of being glad the children are raised in a family filled with love, onlookers' immediate concern is that the children are going to be corrupted and confused.

Every day we are inundated with messages that encourage and reinforce heterosexuality. This is not always done consciously; it is an accumulation of innocent signals and assumptions. A new parent might talk about how her baby boy "flirts" with women. A late-night talk-show host eggs on a little-boy movie-star guest to talk about his "girl-friend." It's assumed that prom dates will be opposite-sex couples, and when young people challenge that assumption, it makes headlines.

A gay man who mentions his "boyfriend" in a casual conversation at work could be considered to be "flaunting" his sexuality. ("I found that movie to be pretty boring, but my boyfriend loved it.") But when a straight man mentions a girlfriend or wife in the same context, it is hardly viewed as an "in your face" declaration of his heterosexuality; it is simply small talk about what he did over the weekend.

A wedding is the most obvious expression of someone's sexuality, and all of the ritual surrounding it celebrates not just sexuality but also sexual *behavior*. Bachelor parties encourage men to "get it out of their system" before they commit to a wife. A "Just Married" sign on the back of a vehicle leaves little doubt in anyone's mind as to what we expect the bride and groom will be doing that evening.

If heterosexuals were asked to "keep it to themselves," it would mean the elimination of any custom or conversation that reveals heterosexuality. No wedding announcements, no mention to anyone about husbands, wives, or their biological children for that matter, since that would indicate a person has been sexually active. No kissing on TV. No public displays of affection. Ever. It would mean hiding, sneaking around, and lying. Seems ridiculous, right? Yet that is what is asked of LGBT people when they are expected not to be open about their sexuality.

Why Do People Need to Come Out to Their Children?

It is exhausting to always have to be "on" as a closeted person, censoring oneself in order not to be "found out." When LGBT people stay in the closet, they must draw on precious emotional energy to pretend to be people they are not. While some people can maintain the facade of the closet longer than others, the authenticity of the parent-child relationship is compromised. Noelle Howey, 30, was fourteen when she learned her father was transgender. She says her relationship with her dad had been unraveling, and that her dad's coming-out was the beginning of repairing that relationship:

> My father was closeted, and being closeted creates this really weird petri dish for all sorts of negativity and self-hatred and hostility. It's such an unnatural way to live that it creates a really negative environment for you and for everyone around you. That's what happened with my dad, so *that's* what we had to get past. We didn't have to get past the fact that she wanted to wear women's clothes and later on that she wanted to become a woman. That was never really an issue for me.[8]

Many children endure the "petri dish for all sorts of negativity" without understanding what is at the root of the tension in their family. During the time that my dad was not out and still living with my mom, he was distant and uptight, and had unpredictable outbursts of anger. I barely had a relationship with him, so when he moved out, I welcomed his departure. After my parents separated, Dad became a new person. The energy he had put into hiding his identity was redirected into being our dad. While most people assumed I would want my mom and dad back together, I preferred a relaxed and attentive father in another house over a mean father living in the same house.

Coming out means putting a stop to all that wasted energy so that a parent can focus on what is most important: parenting.

Katje Hempel, 23, felt similar tension with her father, but he did not come out until Katje was nineteen. "My dad and I didn't have the best relationship before he came out," she remembers. "We didn't communicate at all. I didn't see him enjoying having a family in the slightest. He was spending so much time trying to hide who he was."

Katje's story and those of other children whose parents came out later in life show how parent-child relationships are adversely affected by closeted parents. These parents tend to avoid emotional intimacy with their children because close relationships are more likely to lead to children discovering the secret. These children notice the emotional distance but do not understand why it exists. In the most serious circumstances, the cost of being closeted manifests itself in substance abuse and suicidal thoughts. Noelle talks about her father's behavior and the destructive road her father appeared to be taking:

> When she was a man she drank to excess frequently, was very mean to my mother, and pretty much ignored me. So by the time I was fourteen, she was not my favorite person. I wouldn't have a dad if she hadn't come out. I don't know if she would still be alive, but she certainly wouldn't be accessible to me, emotionally or otherwise. We wouldn't be in touch, probably. So I'm extremely grateful for the fact that she's out.

Some parents take on their own don't-ask-don't-tell policy. They don't consider themselves to be "in" the closet, but they haven't said anything to their kids about it. However, by not discussing it, and therefore not giving the children permission to ask questions, children take the silence as an indication that the topic is off-limits or that they are not supposed to know.

COMMON CONCERNS PARENTS HAVE
ABOUT COMING OUT
OR "WHY I HAVEN'T TOLD MY KIDS YET"

All kinds of circumstances shape a parent's decision about why and when to come out. If you are a parent who has not yet come out to your children, you probably have some major concerns that have convinced you to put it off. Remember that many parents have faced the same situation and emerged triumphant. As you consider the "when" for your own coming-out, you might see part of your experience in this list of things parents commonly say about why they stay in the closet, along with the reality behind their concerns.

Concern: "My sexuality is none of their business. I'm not about to talk to my children about what I do in bed."

The impact of having a gay parent is not inherently negative. As part of a family unit, however, a parent must know that his or her sexual orientation *will* affect the entire family in some way. No matter how much LGBT people want to believe that coming out should be a nonissue, it has an impact on their children, their spouse (if they are married), and their own parents and extended family.

The last thing a parent wants is for anything—any choice or any action—to affect his or her children in a negative way. To acknowledge that a parent's sexual orientation could result in their children facing even slight adversity is territory no parent wants to explore. To some parents, the fear of a negative impact is an acceptable reason to stay closeted to their children.

Parents who are repelled by the idea of discussing their sexual behavior with their children must understand the important distinction between coming out and talking about one's sex life. There is a common misperception that talking to children about sexual orientation automatically means having to talk about sexual activity. This is simply not true. Telling children that Mommy has special feelings for women in the way that some other mommies have special feelings for men, for example, will help children understand why their new "aunt" has moved in. It will not, however, introduce overtly sexual concepts any more than would an early discussion about "the birds and the bees." While coming out to your homo-hesitant coworker might give him an instant mental picture of you in bed with someone of the same sex, younger children do not make the same cognitive leap.

Concern: "I'm waiting until my children are old enough to fully understand these issues."

As I have mentioned, if kids are told when they are young, and before they fully understand what sexuality is, they are less likely to have developed homophobic views that will make it harder for them to accept their parents' sexuality.

Monica was seventeen and her sister was four when their father came out as transgender. Monica says that her sister's young age worked to her advantage:

> When we were sitting at the kitchen table coloring, she said, "You know, some people are girls on the inside and girls on the outside, like us. Some people are girls on the inside and boys on the outside, like Daddy." I remember at the time thinking she's so lucky that she can understand this so easily. It was so much harder for me to process it after already learning what a boy is and what a girl is, and not having any experience with transgender people at all. But my sister was just like, "This is how it is."

When Bruce, a gay dad, came out to his son, the ten-year-old didn't believe him. "It was interesting because he kept saying 'you don't look it,'" Bruce explained. "I asked him what he meant but he couldn't express himself." Bruce brought up the gay-themed sit-com *Will & Grace*, which he and his son occasionally watched together. He mentioned that the suit-wearing lawyer character Will was gay, which was surprising to his son. Then Bruce mentioned the show's more flamboyant character: "I said, 'Jack is gay, too,' and my son said, 'Well, yeah, I know *that*.'" Bruce initially thought he would wait to come out when his son was older, but now says, "I am glad I told him now, because he was already developing preconceived notions about how a gay person looks and acts."

When I was a very young child, I did not have a concept of gay stereotypes, so my father's coming-out did not seem shocking or shameful. From my simple five-year-old perspective, my dad was with someone who made him happy, and that person happened to be a man.

It's never too early to be honest.

Concern: "My ex will use the information against me in a custody battle."

The United States court system has an appalling history of decisions that deny competent parents rights to their children simply because of their sexual orientation. While this trend is changing in many parts of the country, there are other areas where blatant bigotry still exists. For example, in early 2002 the Alabama Supreme Court decided in favor of a heterosexual father's custody of his three children over his former wife, who is lesbian, by a margin of 9–0. In his opinion, Chief Justice Roy Moore wrote, "The common law designates homosexuality as an inherent evil," and concluded that being gay would be reason enough to declare a parent unfit. "The effect of such a lifestyle upon children must not be ignored, and the lifestyle should never be tolerated."[9]

For parents who are in jurisdictions where disclosure of their sexual orientation could likely be exploited to a heterosexual parent's advantage, it is probably safer to come out after custody arrangements have been settled. Legal advice on this matter should be obtained from an attorney or from organizations such as Lambda Legal or the National Center for Lesbian Rights, which are included in Appendix B. (Co-parenting with a former spouse is addressed in the next chapter.)

Concern: "I'm waiting for the right time."

If you are waiting for the right time, ask yourself when that would be. Often parents are not sure about the right time, only that the moment will present itself sometime in the future and will guarantee a problem-free coming-out process. There are no such guarantees.

Parents who tell their children they are getting a divorce often worry that also telling their children one of their parents is gay will be too much information to cope with all at once. In truth, finding out that a parent's sexual orientation is the reason for the divorce can be a great relief. It is the lack of information that causes anxiety in these family situations, because what children conjure up in their minds is often worse than the reality.

Parents who wait for the right time risk the children finding out in the worst ways, namely walking in on a closeted parent during an intimate moment with a lover. After all, if children think a parent's lover is only a "friend," they don't have reason to knock before entering a room, or call before coming home early from a friend's house.

"I wanted to know why my sister and I weren't informed at an earlier time," says Adam. "They said that they were trying to decide the best way to tell my sister and me, but I walked in on them before that day came to pass. I think I held on to this resentment for many years."

Some parents decide to wait until their adolescent children are older, believing that the teen years are the worst time to deal with a parent coming out. But by *not* coming out, parents avoid talking about what the kids might already suspect. Even when children are at an awkward adolescent stage, a parent's coming-out process sets an example of personal integrity at a time when kids are forming their own value systems. Additionally, if they are struggling with issues of their own sexuality (as most teens are, to some extent), a parent's coming-out can give them permission to be more open, too.

Concern: "I have always been 'out.' I don't need to point this out to my kids; doing so makes a bigger deal out of it than it really is."

When parents have been in a same-sex relationship since before the children were born or since they were very small, it is true that their kids have never known it to be any other way. Most likely the children have realized how their family is different, but they might still struggle to find the words to articulate it—especially if their parents don't talk about it with them. They may be confused by homophobic messages they overhear and not know how to respond, or they wonder if their parents would want them to say anything at all.

One lesbian mother told me that even though her six-year-old son is being raised with same-sex parents and is surrounded by other children with similar families, the homophobia still challenges his perspective. When she told him that she was heading off to a gathering of gay parents, he asked, "You mean the *good* kind of 'gay,' right, Mom?" Her son had already heard the word "gay" used as an insult, but also knew his mom and other parents around him were gay. Like many children in these families, he was certain that there were two kinds of gay people: people like his parents, and then those unseemly characters described by homo-hostile people.

Les Addison, 35, was six when her adoptive mother and her mother's partner began living together. While Les understood that her mother and Annette had a relationship, she says that the lack of discussion around the issue left her trying to figure things out on her own:

They could have done much better [in coming out to me]. I could have been given language to use to describe both my relationship to Annette and her relationship to my mother. I was the one who started calling [Annette] my mother, "second mother," or stepmother. I would have liked an explanation about sexual orientation and homophobia in an age-appropriate way . . . as well as information about how it was not understood by other people so that it was something to be kept quiet in certain settings.

Parents who are already out cannot assume their children are equipped with the proper tools, knowledge, or vocabulary simply because it is all the children have ever known. Talking about an LGBT parent's sexual orientation gives children the words to articulate their family to others, and lets them know who they can tell if they choose. It helps to give children specifics, for example: "Because your papa and I love each other and we are both men, most people would say we are 'gay,' or 'homosexual.' We're okay with you telling your friends that your parents are gay."

Concern: "If my children really wanted to know, they would ask. Besides, I don't know how to bring it up."

It is not fair to place the burden of bringing it up on the kids. If a parent is having a difficult time discussing sexuality, how can a child be expected to figure out how to talk about it? Additionally, if a child suspects a parent is gay, but is not certain, the child might worry that the parent will be angry or offended by this assumption.

Even if a child already knows, she might not be sure if she is supposed to know, and she certainly doesn't know if she is allowed to talk about it—with the parent or anyone else. A fifteen-year-old girl explains the difficulty of living with a truth that is unspoken:

My dad and his lover moved in together when I was seven years old and it was really cool and everything. My dad's lover had two kids and it was all cool. We were one big family, but my dad has never told me that he is gay. And so I know it, but he's never discussed it with me. We went to Pride and we marched on Washington [for LGBT equality]. We've watched *Torch Song Trilogy*, but he never came out to me personally.

Since her father has never actually told her, this teen feels like it's a "huge barrier" in her ability to have open communication with her dad. She says that she wishes she could talk to him about the harassment she faces at school because of her family, but she does not feel as though she has permission to acknowledge it. If parents need ideas about how to bring up the topic, they don't need to look very far. They can refer to specific news stories, ads, or movies, and start the conversation from there. Parents can ask their kids what they think about students suing a school board for their right to have a gay-straight alliance, or laws that ban gay people from adopting, or the local LGBT Pride celebration.

It's important to speak honestly and openly, without inundating kids with extra information that they might not understand or might not care to know. They do not need to hear the answers to questions that other people such as therapists, grandparents, or former spouses are asking. Nor do they need to hear all the details about how their parent figured it out or about the parent's sexual activity with a partner or lovers. I have yet to meet *any* child who wants to know the specifics about a parent's sex life.

Concern: *"If my children are not immediately accepting of me after I come out, I fear they will never be supportive."*

The time it takes for a person to come out to oneself can vary greatly. It could take a week or it could take four or more decades. Likewise, family members need to be allowed time to process the information. Laurie Cicotello, 32, who has a transgender father, has talked to many transgender parents whose children are having a hard time accepting their parents' identity. She says that parents often overlook the fact that their own process of accepting themselves was gradual, and that their children's process is also likely to be gradual. "Parents may have to wait the same amount of time for their kids to accept them," Laurie says. "It's kind of brutal, but they expect us to accept them on some time frame that they—or a therapist or a book—has predetermined."

Children's feelings often change once they have had time to think about it and as they mature. Adam, who remembers his initial reaction, at the age of twelve, as "disgust," now has a different perspective on his mother's relationship. "I completely accept it and am happy they are together because they are great together and are happy." His view on same-sex relationships in general has also changed, and he has learned that "*people* matter, not ideas about how people 'should' express their sexual orientation." He adds, "I feel that we are all quite tight now."

When a child's first impulse is to cut off communication with a newly out parent, it usually involves a temporary adjustment period. What a child says in a flurry of emotions one night probably will not hold true ten years from now, or maybe even next week. If communication continues to suffer over a period of several months or even years, a family therapist can serve as a neutral party as parents and children work through this issue. While the therapist does not necessarily have to be LGBT, it is essential that the therapist be LGBT-friendly. Children who are uncomfortable with homosexuality will probably prefer a therapist who they know is not gay so that they don't feel the therapist is on the parent's "side."

TAKING INVENTORY BEFORE COMING OUT
TO CHILDREN

Because every coming-out story is as unique as each family, looking at how your children have gathered information about sexuality in general can give you a sense of the level of understanding and acceptance they might have when you come out. Here are some issues to think about with regard to who or what is influencing them:

Role models. Do you have family or friends you respect who are already out? If you do, plan on incorporating them into your talk. ("Remember how we talked about our neighbors Jim and Chris?") Even though your coming-out might be a surprise to your children, if they know other people who are LGBT, they will be less likely to consider gay people as weird or abnormal and therefore more likely to accept the news.

Attitudes of former spouse. Even if your relationship with your children's other parent is rocky, do you have your former spouse's support in telling them the truth? A spouse who is openly homo-hostile will compound the confusion. A spouse who is supportive can help children accept the information more readily.

Media. What images of gay people have your children seen in the media? These shape their view significantly, particularly if the children do not know any gay people personally. Have they seen movies with gay and lesbian characters that go against the stereotypes? Have they watched news reports about gay rights?

Religion. What have been the attitudes of both the institution and the individuals at your place of worship? Has sexuality been integrated into your religious community in a healthy way, or is it presented as shameful, with no room for discussion? Are there openly LGBT people in the congregation? In roles of leadership?

School and peers. Have there been any lessons on diversity or acceptance at school? Are LGBT-themed books welcome in the school library, or have homophobic parents demanded they be removed from the shelves? Do you hear your children and their friends liberally use the expression "That's so gay"? Does your child have friends who have come out as queer?

Your attitude about LGBT issues. Sometimes the most deeply closeted individuals are the ones who speak out the loudest *against* homosexuality. I've met many children whose parents were unusually vocal about the sinfulness of homosexuality and the need for people to "change" to become heterosexual. Typically, it was their own struggle against gay feelings that caused them to reject homosexuality so passionately. They prayed that their devotion to this view would "save" them. When such parents come out, it can shake the foundation of their children's value system since this system includes the deeply held anti-gay beliefs their parents taught them.

QUESTIONS CHILDREN MIGHT ASK

Some children have lots of questions after a parent comes out. Others don't ask any at all. Some will have questions only after they have thought about it for a while. If you are preparing to come out to your children, here are some of the common questions to anticipate.

"Is this a secret? Who else knows?"

When a parent comes out as LGBT, their family needs to understand how open they can be about it. This is particularly important if you live in a state where antidiscrimination laws do not include sexual orientation (i.e., a homophobic boss who does not want any gay employees can fire someone with impunity). Your feelings about whom it is okay to tell might change with job transfers or after certain relatives pass away. Children will need to know about those changes.

If your children are the only people you are out to, they might feel that you have simply passed the burden of secrecy on to them. "My dad came out to me, but was not willing to come out to the whole world," remembers Nikkie, 26. "He told me not to talk to anyone. He made me a guard to his closet, and that was not, and still is not, a good position to be in. I don't think you should come out to your children unless you are willing to come out to the world."

Ideally, you have a network of people whom you trust and whom your children trust. These people could include your parents, your former spouse, a teacher at school, or someone in the neighborhood. Some children are more comfortable asking the tough questions of an adult other than you. Regardless of how your former spouse accepts or rejects you, it is important that your children are not required to keep this secret from their other parent, nor should they be expected to tell their other parent on your behalf. Take care of this issue before you tell your kids.

"Does this mean I'm gay, too?"

The tone in which you answer this question will leave a lasting impression on your children. Answer calmly and without being defensive. I have known too many parents whose knee-jerk reaction has been to say, "Oh, no, no, no, no! My being gay has nothing to do with you!" or "No! *I'm* gay. *You* will be straight." The message sent by such defensive responses is that you would be disappointed if they were anything but straight. Instead, try something like, "It could be that you will have special feelings for men or women or both. That's something only you can figure out for yourself. Whatever you grow up to be, I just want you to be happy. And I will always love you."

"Will we get kicked out of our religious community?"

Kids of nearly every age have already heard religious extremists who hiss the word "homosexual" as if it were a swear word. Depending on the children's age and level of maturity, they may leap to the conclusion that *all* religions have disdain for gays. Some of their fears, however, could be well founded. Katje recalls how members at their Lutheran church distanced themselves from her family after her dad came out:

> Growing up, we had to go to church every Sunday. My parents were very, very, very strict about that. Then things switched when my dad came out. My parents stopped going to church. I remember going one or two Sundays with my father after he came out. I just remember still being in the space of being angry at my father yet at the same time feeling [protective] of him. Very few people, maybe one or two, came up to talk to him. . . . My parents actually got most of their support from my best friend's father, who was the minister at the Congregational church. It was ironic—because they should have been getting that support from *our* church.

If you attend religious services regularly, talk to your children about the congregation's attitudes about homosexuality, and, if applicable, what is happening to make positive change. Let them know if you are out to other members of the congregation, or if you are considering finding another community where the family will feel more accepted. For information on acceptance in spiritual communities contact Soulforce, an interfaith organization listed in Appendix B.

"Does this mean you are going to hell?"

Children cannot help but hear the continual threat of hell as the place where homosexuals—and this now includes their parents—will be going. So pervasive is this notion, some young children worry about it even when it is outside of their family's belief system. Derek, 33, always knew that his mom was lesbian and that his late father was gay, but it wasn't until he was thirteen that he was officially told. Hearing people use religion to make judgments about homosexuality was difficult for him:

> Growing up in the South, the only thing you heard was that gays and lesbians would go to hell and that their way of life was wrong. This turned me off to religion altogether for a while, until I realized that a lot of people are ignorant on the grounds of religion. I have now grown spiritually and have come to understand that the South was wrong.

If children ask questions about hell or sinning, talk them through their worries, no matter how unrealistic the conversation seems to you. I don't think anyone can underestimate how terrifying it is for young children to wonder if their mommy or daddy will burn in hell.

"Do you have AIDS?"

The less contact your children have had with people who are openly gay, the more likely they are to automatically associate being gay with having AIDS. For people who were educated about AIDS in health classes, it's hard to imagine that such assumptions still exist, but they do. Let your children know that AIDS is something that everyone needs to protect themselves from and that you are making choices that minimize your chances of contracting the virus.

If you *are* living with HIV, your children need to know what steps you are taking to keep yourself healthy, and they need to be reminded of ways that HIV is spread, none of which include living in the same house as someone who is HIV-positive. (This topic is covered more extensively in Chapter Six.)

"Why didn't you tell me earlier? How long have you known?"

This question might have to do with solving some ongoing mysteries, like why there has been so much tension between their parents lately, or why their Christian fundamentalist cousin didn't invite them to Thanksgiving dinner this year. The children might also be ashamed of their own anti-gay comments and try to retrace their steps to figure out what you may have heard. ("Does Mom notice when my teammates call each other fags?" Or: "Why didn't we give the game Smear the Queer a different name like Dad asked us to?")

Children might also want the information in order to understand how closely your coming-out process aligns with the timing of when they began to notice their parent had a secret of some sort. Sean was twenty-one when his dad came out to him as transgender, but Sean, who is now twenty-seven, says he and his sister suspected it for years. His sister's makeup would mysteriously disappear and reappear, and when Sean "ended up poking around my dad's stuff a few times," he discovered women's clothing, makeup, and jewelry. "I'd find little hints that maybe Dad was a cross-dresser or something like that," Sean says. "When he actually told us what was going on, I don't think it was really momentous because we had always figured something was going on all along."

Phillip, 27, also says he "pretty much knew" his mom was lesbian, but she did not officially tell him until he was seventeen:

> I had my suspicions for a while leading up to it. My sister was like me, wondering why our mom waited so long to come out. Mom said there were many reasons, but mostly fear of rejection from her family and friends. I felt like I needed to reassure her that I was supportive of her. I pretty much made that clear right off the bat when she told me.

If your children ask you why you didn't come out earlier, they might also be wondering if you thought they couldn't be trusted with the information. Emphasize that your delay in coming out to them was not a reflection on your relationship or your love for them.

Additional Suggestions for
Coming Out to Children

Consider your timing. Pick a nondescript day when your schedule isn't hectic and stress levels are relatively low. If you come out on a birthday or major holiday, the day might forever be remembered as the Day Mom Came Out. National Coming Out Day—October 11—can be the extra push some people need, but it does not have to mean "now or never." Be sensitive to what is going on in your family members' lives. For example, if you have a child who is studying for an exam that is scheduled for the following day, hold off until the weekend.

Come out on their territory. I've heard too many stories in which parents bring this topic up in the car. I don't recommend this; life-changing information is dangerous at fifty-five miles an hour. Other less-than-desirable locations are a relative's home (where children might feel trapped and required to be on their best behavior) and at a restaurant or other public setting where natural and spontaneous reactions (like yelling or tears) are not considered appropriate. Anywhere but home might leave children feeling like they are cornered, or that you're deliberately trying to suppress a dramatic outburst.

Don't send a messenger. The children should hear it from you before they hear it from anyone else. If they also have a straight parent who is willing to be with you when you tell them, that can be a helpful way to let the children know that they won't have to pick sides. But if the straight parent tells them when you are not there, it can add to the confusion. Kirk Wisland, 30, learned that his father was gay from his mother and stepfather. "At age nine I wasn't really grasping what it meant anyway," says Kirk, "but I remember that I actually built up some resentment toward my mom and my stepfather for telling me this. I felt like they were somehow attacking my father."

Telling your children yourself also lets them know that you are not ashamed and that you are willing to answer their questions. Kirk adds,

"I guess, looking back, I wish that they would have set it up so that my dad was telling me, even if my mom and my stepdad had wanted to be there, too."

Know that a wide range of reactions is possible. Your children might be speechless, they might yell at you, they might cry or even laugh. When Emily Hansen's father told her and her brother that he was gay, she cried. "Tears of shock more than anything," says Emily, 23. At the same time her brother was laughing. "I am not sure either one of us really believed what we had just heard."

Some reactions are delayed until children are old enough to comprehend that their parents' sexuality is connected to social stigma. Joe Hake, 22, says his mother's relationship with her partner was initially a nonissue in their family. Joe's little brother was told that his mom was gay and did not have a problem with it until he was about eight years old and a kiss between his mom and her partner upset him.

"He just knew that girls weren't supposed to kiss girls," says Joe. "He didn't know what 'gay' meant, he just knew it was wrong. . . . When he finally put it together that it meant they were gay, he started crying."

As children go through developmental stages, new questions will come up and new challenges will arise. Make sure your children know that they can talk to you or another adult they trust whenever they need or want to.

Never give up. If the worst-case scenario—your children rejecting you—happens, make every effort to stay in contact with them. It might be tempting to try to minimize the pain of rejection by giving up. But their rejection of you does not warrant you—the parent—to reject them as well. Send cards, make phone calls, and let them know that you are always open to resuming your relationship. Even the most reticent children talk about becoming more open as they get older, especially after they move out on their own and develop their own views and opinions. A thirty-two-year-old daughter from the Midwest thought her relationship with her mother was beyond repair when her mother came out:

> I was extremely homophobic when I was sixteen and I was terrified. The divorce, my mom coming out—all within three months. I was very resentful and I'm not proud of my behavior. I was terrible to my mother. My mom and I didn't talk for a year when I went to college. And it was her insistence to stay in my life and the way she doggedly pursued me with letters and packages and phone calls. When you realize that the world doesn't end, that gay and lesbian people are just like you, things get better. It was definitely a journey for me.

Katje, who had a nearly nonexistent relationship with her father before he came out, says that despite the rocky coming-out process, her relationship with her father is the strongest it has ever been:

> If you had told me five years ago that this kind of relationship would be going on with my dad, I wouldn't have believed you. I probably would have laughed. I remember, when I was younger, craving for my dad to be in communication with me the way he is now. He's trying so hard it's adorable. I totally love and embrace him.

If you and your children are estranged, they need to know your love for them is not conditional on their acceptance of you. Don't give up hope that over time the shock will wear off. Make sure they know you will be readily available when it does. Otherwise, they might be so ashamed of their behavior that they think that you would not want to see them again. When they do come around, as more time passes, they might even forget that they were ever anything but supportive.

I wish I could hand parents the secret recipe for a perfect coming-out process, but there is none. Every family is unique in circumstances, personalities, and outside pressures, all of which contribute to how children react to the news. Coming out is not a one-time event; it is an ongoing process. With time and compassion, opening the closet door also opens the door to better communication between children and their parents.

Three
Family Change: Supporting Children Through Divorces and Same-Sex Breakups

Living with divorced parents, especially gay parents, was not very easy. But living with any divorced parents is not easy.
—TABBY DYE, 20

In my last week of high school, my mother and father joined me at a luncheon to honor graduating seniors. Afterward, I introduced Mom and Dad to one of my teachers, who congratulated them for doing such a great job raising me. My parents beamed and Mr. Hall beamed back. He said he hoped they wouldn't mind if he claimed just a little bit of the credit for helping their daughter turn out so well. He told my parents that I provided some hope for him, because as time passed he was feeling more discouraged about the future for his students. "You've clearly provided the support Abby needs to make it in this world," Mr. Hall told them. "It's too bad so many kids just don't have a fighting chance. But what can you expect from children who come from *broken homes*."

After he walked away, the three of us looked at one another and giggled about passing as a white-picket-fence family. I did not mean to deceive my teacher; I just never had a reason in his classroom to mention that my mom and dad had been divorced for twelve years. Mr.

Hall saw what he wanted to see based on his values and assumptions. Since I did not demonstrate behavior that Mr. Hall associated with a "broken home," he assumed my mom and dad were still married.

In the midst of my father officially coming out and my parents getting divorced, they made a conscious choice to make parenting a priority over their marital crisis. During this painful time in both of their lives, Mom and Dad supported my brother and me, and still encouraged us to have a relationship with the other parent instead of hoping we would pick sides. They agreed to joint custody without dispute. Despite the dearth of information in the late 1970s to help my mother come to terms with her husband's sexuality, she ignored the societal assumption that my father would be unfit to raise us because he was gay.

When I became active in the LGBT-family community nearly a decade ago, most of the families involved were headed by same-sex couples who became parents through adoption or donor insemination. These parents maintained a hopeful assumption that the dawn of the "gayby boom" also marked the end of the time when children with gay parents had to experience divorce. Unlike LGBT people whose children were the result of heterosexual marriages, same-sex parents do not need to worry about sexual orientation ending the relationship. Unfortunately, some same-sex couples are facing the reality of divorce for many reasons other than incompatible sexual orientations. Although gay marriage is not legal in the United States, the emotional, social, and financial changes that accompany same-sex breakups make them "divorces" in every sense but the legal one.

Many of the issues that affect children of same-sex breakups overlap with issues that affect children who experience heterosexual divorces. Feeling caught in the middle with parents and extended family, being vulnerable to losing a parent in custody cases, and having to integrate new "stepparents" into their lives perplex children of divorce no matter their parents' orientations.

Divorces do not always have dramatic stories attached to them, but these are the ones we hear most often. Children from unremark-able divorces find it hard to explain how their parents minimized the drama. They skim over the experience, only mentioning what was ab-sent: they did not hear fighting, they were not expected to pick sides, and the extended family of one parent did not disparage the other.

When my dad moved into Russ's house and I went back and forth between houses without debate, I did not realize that some kids were not so fortunate. I took for granted how well my parents handled co-parenting until I started hearing more difficult stories from other chil-dren. Some cannot remember a time when their parents exchanged a civil word with each other. Now that I am an adult, I understand that my accepting attitude about my family was mainly due to how Mom and Dad helped me frame my thinking about the divorce. Our family was not "broken"; it was simply changing. Divorce was part of that ex-perience, but it was not a tragic ending.

MARRIED AND COMING OUT

When a mother and father split up because one of them comes out, the process is rarely simple. These couples are what Amity Pierce Bux-ton, Ph.D., calls "mixed-orientation marriages." She founded the Straight Spouse Network in the early 1990s and is the author of *The Other Side of the Closet: The Coming-Out Crisis for Straight Spouses and Families*. Dr. Buxton, whose former husband came out as gay, estimates that there are up to two million marriages in the United States in which one of the spouses turns out to be lesbian, gay, bisexual, or transgender. Not all LGBT people who are married will come out to their spouses.

As homosexuality gradually loses its societal stigma, more people will be able to come out to themselves before they feel pressure to enter into a heterosexual marriage. Still, some LGBT people continue to get married for various reasons. Some are not fully aware of their sexuality before they marry. Some believe that with a lot of prayer and faith they will "change." Others want to be a parent so badly and they are not familiar or not comfortable with alternative ways to have children.

Some children find out their parents got married already knowing one of them felt same-sex attractions. In some of these families, the couple believed getting married would "make" the gay parent straight. Other couples chose to go ahead and get married because they thought the strong connection of friendship and shared values was a higher priority than sexual attraction.

Families adapt to a parent coming out in a variety of ways. Some parents immediately divorce, while others negotiate an open marriage where one or both spouses are permitted to date other people. Others choose to wait until a child finishes high school or college, or may not feel the need to "act" on anything right away, even though a same-sex sexual relationship may be a long-term goal. Other couples initially intend to stay together, but as time passes, they find that they cannot, either because the tensions become too much or because circumstances change.

"My parents planned to stay together," says Katje Hempel, 23, about her father's coming-out five years ago. "Jessi and I actually facilitated a conversation between the two of us and my parents." Her sister Jessi, 27, explains:

> We called them on a conference call. We told them, "We are your children and we need to make a few things clear. We can't take on your burdens. We need to know you're okay. We think you should divorce, and we know it will be on your time. We don't want to know the axis of your crisis; we just

need to know that you are okay. We want to know that you have good therapists. But we really can't deal."

The conversation helped Jessi and Katje set boundaries with their parents while giving them a chance to express how the tension between their parents was affecting them. Jessi says it also made her see how the parent-child emotional roles had been reversed. "It's a conversation I'm still mad we had to have because ultimately they are our parents. It felt turned around; like *we* were the parents." Katje adds, "We helped our parents get divorced. Looking back on it now, it is truly comical. But at the time, it was a mess."

Marriages that are most likely to remain intact are those in which a spouse comes out as bisexual, but the love and sexual attraction the couple shares remain unchanged. In such instances, coming out is a way of acknowledging their attraction to both men and women, but in terms of their behavior, bisexual spouses may decide to remain monogamous. In this way, bisexual people can resemble married heterosexual couples. For example, a heterosexual married man will feel attraction to women besides his wife, but that does not automatically mean he will have an affair.

Couples in which a spouse comes out as transgender may also decide to remain married. Laurie Cicotello's mother and father married in 1969 and have lived as a legally married same-sex couple since her father came out as transgender in 1985. Reflecting on her parents' choice to stay together, Laurie, 32, says:

> My parents talked about getting divorced from the time I was in the third grade, but a lot changed and now they are tight. I personally would not have stayed in the marriage the way my mom did. Well, of course I say that, but I still haven't experienced a romantic relationship I couldn't or wouldn't walk

away from. I hope one day I am in a relationship that is so solid that if I had to question that, I would choose to stay regardless.

People in mixed-orientation marriages often find they are open to options they never thought they would have considered before they were actually in the situation. There is no single "right" way for couples to handle the restructuring of the family when a parent comes out. Regardless of how parents choose to respond to the family change, the children deserve to maintain quality relationships with both their mom and dad. Children need both their parents to cooperate in order to support them during and after the parents' separation.

SUPPORTING STRAIGHT SPOUSES

How straight spouses react after the disclosure has a profound effect on how their children feel about the divorce, their straight parent, and their LGBT parent. For the newly out person, there can be a mix of emotions: relief, excitement and anticipation, not to mention feelings of guilt for hurting the heterosexual spouse. Learning that a spouse is LGBT is devastating news for someone who truly believed the commitment to a husband or wife would be "until death do us part."

Since this book focuses on the perspective of the children, a full discussion of the perspectives of heterosexual husbands and wives in mixed-orientation marriages is outside of its scope. However, it is critical that straight parents have the support and resources they need so their feelings of shock, anger, or betrayal are not funneled into custody fights, or tension that leaves children feeling stuck in the middle. If the feelings of straight spouses are trivialized, or they are expected to "move on" immediately, their isolation can lead to angry and vocal opposition. This is especially dangerous when straight parents are already homophobic; learning that their spouse is gay will only serve to reinforce their homophobia.

When there are children involved, the angry straight parent could pass homophobia on to the children. This is easy for parents to do, since young minds are receptive to internalizing what their parents teach them. One adult son explained how, while rebuilding a relationship with his estranged gay father, he realized the extent of the homophobia he learned from his mother. She had led him to believe that homosexuals were "filthy," a belief so ingrained that he felt uncomfortable as a guest in his father's home. While rationally he knew his father was not unclean, the son was in his thirties before he could dismiss the prejudice he had internalized from his mother decades earlier.

Straight parents who deeply oppose homosexuality justify sharing their anti-gay attitudes with their children as a way to "balance" what the gay parent is teaching by example—that homosexuality is acceptable. One straight wife told me that her husband could have stayed married if he had really been committed, and that his attraction to men was the result of his inability to stave off deviant behavior. She believed that as the mother of her children, she had a right to pass on her values to her children so that they would know "right from wrong," heterosexuality being, in her view, right and homosexuality wrong.

"I don't say their dad is a bad person," the mother explained. "I say, 'Your dad has a problem, just like people who are alcoholic or addicted to cocaine.'" Even though the mother's intent is to let her kids know that she does not condone homosexuality, expressing this view to children whose father is gay is not fair. An eight-year-old is going to be confused if his mom tells him that his father—half of his biological composition— has feelings that are the equivalent of a cocaine addiction.

To learn that a straight parent does not approve of the other parent being gay is very upsetting to children who are already dealing with homophobic attitudes in the rest of their everyday lives. Robyn's mother's disapproval of her gay dad had a direct effect on how comfortable she felt communicating with her mother. Robyn, 27, remembers one incident when, after spending the day with her dad, she began to relay a funny story to her mom that she heard from her dad's partner. Her mother glared at her and said she "didn't need to hear about it." Robyn recalls how her mother's reaction affected her:

> Until then it had not occurred to me that my own mom would have such a negative reaction to my dad's sexuality. . . . I can understand now the pain he likely caused her by coming out, but as a child, I could not bear that she could be one of those homophobic people that I was so afraid of encountering in public, and that in my own house I wasn't free to discuss his "real" identity. I took her insult toward him very personally, and from then on I avoided discussing almost anything involving my dad with my mother.

Hearing homophobic sentiment from a straight parent does not just threaten a child's relationship with his gay parent. It also builds a barrier between the child and the angry straight parent.

Some straight parents adjust faster than others, which facilitates a smoother adjustment to the divorce for the children. Phillip, 27, says that he was fortunate that his straight dad never pressured him to choose sides. Phillip was seventeen, old enough to appreciate the effort his father made in minimizing the tensions that could have come with Phillip's mom coming out. Phillip explains:

> It wasn't ugly at all. I remember thinking how I would feel if I were married and the person I was married to left me for another woman. I remember thinking I would be more torn up

about it than if she had left for another guy. I don't know what
the rationale behind that is, probably just a knee-jerk macho
reaction. From what I picture of divorces, this one was pretty
smooth. They actually hang out now. They have remained
good friends, which is fantastic, I think.

Although considering the feelings of the straight parent might be
painful for the parent who is coming out, recognizing the straight
spouse's hurt helps rebuild mutual respect. It enables the couple to
communicate effectively about post-disclosure issues—most impor-
tantly, co-parenting. LGBT people who are married and have come
out to their spouse (or plan to) commonly try to avoid thinking about
how the straight spouse will be affected. They prefer to avoid stirring
up feelings of guilt and blame for ending the marriage, which is usually
what the person was trying to delay by not coming out in the first
place. But having empathy for straight spouses brings with it the benefit of minimizing hostility between the couple in the long run and re-
ducing the feelings of homophobia the straight spouse might have.
When mixed-orientation couples commit to a mutually respectful relationship after the shock of disclosure, their children are able to have
more stable and consistent relationships with them both.

When straight spouses do not get the support they need, they
harbor anger and resentment. Their feelings of betrayal remain unresolved and the tension affects the entire family. Heather, 26, says
that even though it has been twenty years since her parents divorced,
her mother is "still hung up on my dad wanting to become a woman."
Her mother's adamant refusal to be in the same room with Heather's
father meant that she did not attend her daughter's wedding.

"I'm so mad about that," Heather says. "I just wanted to tell her,
'This is not about you for once. Would you think about me for a
minute? You've put me second to your wounds and your victim role for

the past twenty years. And I'd like it for this once if you could suck it up and be my mom.'"

Heather did not tell her mom what she really wanted to say, because she knows how hurt her mother still feels. At the same time, however, she was not going to uninvite her father. Heather came up with what she thought was a mature compromise: the offer to hold a special private celebration with her mother. Heather was stunned when her mother responded, "But that means he won."

"What does that mean?" Heather wondered. "Dad 'won'? This is not some game."

Heather recently learned about the Straight Spouse Network. Even though she knows she cannot make her mother work through the issues that remain barriers to their relationship, she wishes her mother would get the support she needs. "I want to get my mom on that website or get her a book or something," she says. "Maybe if she just did not feel so isolated, she would make some progress for the sake of her kids."

Most children hope at minimum that their parents will be able to act cordially toward each other at important family events like weddings and graduations. Some divorced parents surprise even their children when they are able to build a new friendship after emotional wounds heal. David Wells, 28, was two years old when his dad came out and his parents divorced. He can't remember what it was like when his mom and dad were in the same house. He does, however, remember the arguments and tension throughout his childhood, and says he's grateful that they tapered off by the time he was a teenager. Recently David's mom relocated to Minneapolis and is staying with her former husband while she looks for a place of her own. It's an arrangement that would have been unimaginable to David when he was a child. "Mom was very hurt for a very long time," he says. "But I know they had a deep connection with each other and that helped them work though their differences."

By pursuing support groups, on-line resources, and understanding friends, straight spouses can take care of their emotional needs and, in turn, be more emotionally available to their children. They can also accelerate their children's process of accepting a newly out parent. Straight parents can connect with other parents who have gone through similar experiences through the Straight Spouse Network and through support groups created in partnership with PFLAG.

The opportunity to enlist straight spouses as allies is reason enough to include them in LGBT family outreach and support. Outspoken straight spouses expose the extreme social pressure LGBT people face that causes them to enter into mixed-orientation marriages and hide their sexuality. Their stories also demonstrate how getting married will not make an LGBT person straight. Hearing formerly married gays and their straight former spouses share their stories is an antidote to the "ex-gay" myth—the belief that gay people only need to be dedicated to changing their "lifestyle" in order to be heterosexual.

Gay people who feel tempted to seek the comfort, convenience, or social status of a "traditional" family need to realistically understand the likely consequences of entering into a deceptive marriage. The personal stories told publicly by straight spouses are testaments to why gay people's attempts to "change" by getting married are not only futile, but also grossly unfair.

CUSTODY AFTER A DIVORCE

When there is a custody dispute, some divorcing parents erroneously think they are empowering their children by expecting them to choose which parent they want to live with. Having to make such a choice is too much pressure. Children might be hesitant to choose to live with a gay parent for a variety of reasons, including the shock of the newly disclosed information about their parent's sexuality, or their desire to show loyalty to the straight parent. When children are led to see the gay parent as the "bad" parent, someone who hurt the straight parent, and the person blamed for "leaving," they feel pulled to the straight parent's side. In their minds, they have already had one parent leave; choosing the straight parent is their way to ensure that they don't lose them both.

If straight spouses are already homophobic, their first reaction might be to try to keep the children away from the parent who is homosexual. This reaction could be simply vindictive, or it could be an ignorant yet genuine concern—the result of a lifetime of hearing stereotypes about gay people, and the fear that their children will be adversely affected by their gay parent. These straight spouses think their children should be "sheltered" from having too much contact with the gay parent out of fear that it will be confusing.

Many adult children share remarkably similar memories of straight parents who threatened to use the gay parent's sexual orientation against them in court. They remember living with the fear that the straight parent would carry out the threat at some point. These children heard their straight parent or extended-family members make references to their ability to gain custody if they really wanted to. Hearing this negativity while trying to come to terms with the gay parent's sexuality makes children anxious.

Joe Hake, 22, whose mother came out when he was eight, remembers his straight father trying to convince the children to move in with him. "He never took any legal action," says Joe. "He just kept telling us that there was a judge who had made a public statement that no lesbian was a fit mother."

Kristin Joos, 26, remembers how her straight mother threatened to use her gay father's sexual orientation as leverage in court in order to control visitation rights. "My mom basically threatened my dad," says Kristin. "She said that he had to agree to her terms or she would 'out' him to the court—a very, very conservative Southern judge—and he wouldn't get to see us at all."

In both of these examples, it mattered little that the straight parent never followed up on the threats. It was the ongoing fear of a separation—knowing that a parent was thinking about it and could make it happen—that the children remember.

Knowing how being gay has been used in order to determine custody, gay parents are fearful. For Sandy's mom, this fear triggered an extreme reaction after she came out as lesbian in the 1970s when Sandy was almost three years old. In a panic, her mom ran away, as Sandy, now twenty-seven, explains:

> She was petrified that my dad would take me away and she would never get to see me again. I think she felt like if she took me, she could prevent that. We went up to Canada for a while and then we spent some time in Maine—really secluded places. And then she realized she was making a bad choice. I was asking, "Where's my daddy, where's my daddy?"

Upon their return, custody disputes ensued, which Sandy says were based on questions about which parent could provide her with more stability rather than questions about sexual orientation. By the time she was seven or eight, she was still not old enough to understand everything that was happening, but was able to grasp the concept that she was caught in the middle of their conflict. "There were a couple [of] different incidents," remembers Sandy, "where I felt like I had a choice of never seeing my dad again or never seeing my mom again. Emotionally, it was very stressful and confusing to feel like I had to make one ultimate decision between them."

Samantha Gottlieb, 24, remembers the confusion of custody disputes between her mom and dad in the 1980s. Her mother was awarded custody and her visits to her father's home were allowed only if his partner was not present. Samantha's father appealed and was awarded custody when she was about eight years old. Her mother violated the rules of the agreement, taking her out of the state, until the police eventually caught up to them and Samantha was returned to her father. The custody disputes continued, which included her mother reporting her father to Child Welfare. How many times this occurred Samantha does not recall, but she does remember an investigative visit from police when she was home from school, sick, and her father's partner was taking care of her. She remembers this experience as a "witch-hunt":

> To have someone come in and evaluate, knowing that you're at risk for being taken away, was a horrible feeling. You never know if something you say might be construed as something bad that would take you away. To have a social reprimand constantly battering you is horrible; to realize that what is your safe home could be taken away from you. To have that sense of happiness and wellness destroyed by your own mother is so bizarre. How can you not understand that a child who is six, seven, eight, would be affected?

Her relationship with her mother is strained. "She doesn't own up to forcing me to [leave the state with her]," says Samantha. "She has no conception now that that was not an appropriate action." She has tried to talk to her mother about the long-term impact the childhood drama had on her life, but her mother still feels justified in doing what she did. "That makes me sad," Samantha says, "but I've come to understand that she just isn't going to get it."

As the assumption of the "unfit" gay parent is confronted, custody cases like those of the 1970s and 1980s are becoming less common, but they have by no means disappeared. Theron McGriff, a gay dad from Idaho, is in the middle of a dispute that is reminiscent of Samantha's story. In 2000, after several years of sharing joint custody amicably with the mother of his children, he was surprised when his right to

custody was brought into question because he and his same-sex partner decided to live together. Theron is in the process of appealing a
ruling that says in order to have visitation rights, his same-sex partner
cannot live with him. He says his daughters, ages eight and twelve, are
as frustrated as he is that a judge made the decision based on homophobic assumptions rather than on what would be best for this family
specifically. Theron explains:

> It has devastated us, to have a court say, "You can't be a fam-
> ily." We *are* a family. And like my kids said, "Who has the
> right to tell us who can live here?" I'm a better person and par-
> ent because of my partner. When he's not here, they ask
> where he is. They want him here. . . . [My kids] don't under-
> stand why the judge has never met them. Someone who has
> never met them is making decisions for them. That's the
> biggest thing. They think if they could just get to the judge,
> they could clear this up.

Theron's children spend the majority of their time with their
mother. They are caught in the confusion of loving her yet resenting
her decision to pursue legal action. This has put a strain on their father's finances as well as everyone's emotional energy. Even if Theron
is successful in his appeal, nothing can erase childhood memories
clouded by this custody dispute.

When parents successfully separate their feelings about the divorce from their decisions about custody, they give their children the
gift of security. Orson Morrison, 30, remembers that his mother was
"devastated" when her husband came out, which at first made it difficult for her to be positive about her children's father. "I think underneath it all she still had a lot of emotions," Orson says, "a lot of anger,
a lot of bitterness. . . . For several years after their divorce they didn't

really speak. But then something changed in my mom. She was able to put her issues aside and really encouraged my sister and me to have a relationship with my dad."

Orson's adult perspective on his family's history has helped him gain insight into the choices his mother made to move past their family crisis. Many adult children grow to have an added appreciation for how their parents overcame their conflicts to support their children and avoid the trauma of a custody dispute.

SAME-SEX BREAKUPS

Children with same-sex parents learn lessons about family early on. They know their family is different. They hear the comments about "those kinds of families." Their parents tell them: "We are a family. *Love* makes a family." Children trust the lesson; they believe in it, hoping that the people who think "those kinds of families" are so different will someday believe it, too.

When relationships go sour, sometimes the beautiful mantra "love makes a family" comes with a caveat: love makes a family unless the parent with the most power says otherwise. In this situation, the parent with the most power is the one who has biological or adoptive ties to the children. Depending on the jurisdiction in which the family lives, the parent who is not legally recognized could be reduced to a "roommate" or "baby-sitter," which prevents her from having access to the children that the two parents planned on raising together.

Custody disputes are not, and do not have to be, a standard procedure for every gay couple that splits up, although cases profiled in the media could lead readers to believe otherwise. When media cover same-sex custody disputes, the focus is on the dynamic between the ex-partners. The children, usually protected by the use of their initials or pseudonyms, seem almost hypothetical; symbols of an intriguing twist in the evolution of same-sex relationships. The divorces of same-sex parents are covered only at the point when a court case is involved and the controversy is at its peak.

Media give little or no attention to the other side of gay-parent divorces—the success stories—by virtue of the fact that without a conflict, there is no story. There are plenty of same-sex couples with children who handle their breakups without placing great anxiety on their children. These families have joint custody, or at least regular visitation. These are parents who acknowledge that when a relationship between partners ends, the relationship between a parent and child does not. Other children are less fortunate.

Statistics on same-sex-parent breakups are difficult to gather because unlike the case of heterosexual divorces, such breakups are not recorded through legal filings. But just as in any breakup between heterosexual parents, same-sex parents need to decide what sort of visitation or custody each parent will have. Some couples break up amicably and are able to come up with custody agreements on their own. Others have a much more difficult time, sometimes dragging on a custody battle for years. The irony in these disputes is that the biological parent can use the very system that has denied legal recognition of her family in order to deprive her ex-partner custody of the child.

Lisa Coons-Andersen has a five-year-old daughter she has not seen since she was three. Her former partner gave birth to the child in Florida, but Lisa, the nonbiological parent, is not legally recognized. When their relationship began to deteriorate, the couple tried counseling but ultimately her partner decided to move out. While initially Lisa and her partner adhered to a custody schedule of equal time, as time passed Lisa's contact with her child was decreased from half-time to every other weekend to every three weeks and ultimately, never.

Lisa now maintains a website to connect with other nonbiological parents in similar situations. As she hears stories from other distraught women and compares them to her own experience, she has tried to understand her ex-partner's motivation. Her interest in wanting to be able to see the situation through her former partner's eyes has made her remarkably compassionate. "They truly believe that what they're doing is right," Lisa says about the biological moms who fight for full custody. "They think that it's in the best interest of the child to not deal with extra complications." By "complications," she's referring to living in two households, and having the memory of a painful breakup. Now she wonders if her daughter even remembers her.

Even if a parent who is not legally recognized lives in a state where her case will be heard by a judge, high legal fees affect her ability to pursue the process. Lisa says she hears from other nonbiological moms who have drained their resources, or never had the money in the first place to seek legal representation. "Where do you come up with a two-thousand-dollar retainer?" Lisa wonders. "For so many of these parents, even coming up with the hundred and eighty dollars for an initial consultation [with an attorney] is a struggle."

It would be preferable, both emotionally and financially, if parents did not have to fight for custody through lawyers or court cases. Some families are seeking sensible alternatives.

PLANNING AHEAD, JUST IN CASE

For same-sex couples, overcoming the barrier of *how* to have children can become so consuming that it is nearly impossible to think beyond it. Wrapped up as they are in the excitement and anxiety of becoming parents—of "starting a family"—the last thing a couple wants to consider is what they would do if their relationship were to dissolve.

Prospective parents need to consult a lawyer to learn about the options available to them—in terms of adoption and legal documentation—so that both parents' relationship to the children will be recognized to the full extent of the law. Legal options that are available to families will depend on the state, the county, and in some cases the individual judge's interpretation of laws that were created with no mention of same-sex parents. Some parents even choose to move to a different state, one where both parental relationships are legally recognized. This is not an option available to all families. The financial burden of legal fees and relocation is too great for parents with little or no discretionary income.

Ideally, a couple who decides to split up should keep custody disputes out of court altogether in order to avoid the emotional and financial drain. In "Protecting Families: Standards for Child Custody in Same-Sex Relationships," the Gay & Lesbian Advocates & Defenders in Boston collaborated with LGBT family advocacy organizations to advocate for custody agreements between same-sex parents that honor the family ties that traditional courts do not yet recognize. The collaborative work was created to prevent bitter same-sex parent custody cases like the ones that make headlines. In its introduction, the authors explain the need for such a document: "It is extremely damaging to our community and our families when we disavow as insignificant the very relationships for which we are seeking legal and societal respect."[10]

Jenifer Firestone, LCSW, founder of Alternative Family Matters, has been helping LGBT parents create families together since 1990. Part of her commitment is to help these families make child-centered decisions during times of conflicts that could potentially result in ending the couple's partnership.

Firestone advocates creating a "Family Council" before the first child is even born. This group of problem-solving family members and friends is dedicated to supporting the family, in the form the parents originally intended it to have, and advocating for the children when there are conflicts that threaten the child's relationship with one of the parents. Firestone observes that upon becoming parents, many couples abandon the networks and support available within their communities, presuming that a "nuclear family" can and should be self-sufficient. With the help of a Family Council, a couple can work through issues, attitudes, and emotions that, in the context of a breakup, might cause a biological or legal parent to minimize the status of the other parent.

While many parents find peace of mind in preparing for the worst-case scenario, others are more resistant. Many same-sex couples do not plan ahead for a breakup. They don't do this for some of the same reasons heterosexual couples do not draw up a prenuptial agreement. Some think it is unromantic. Some think it would communicate a lack of trust between them. Others fear it will become a self-fulfilling prophecy: you plan for a breakup and it is bound to happen. And finally, many partners disregard it because they are *certain* they will be together forever.

When Firestone was working with a female couple that was planning to conceive and raise a child together, one of the women expressed her resentment about being urged to develop a co-parenting agreement. Firestone remembers the prospective mother's reaction:

> She got furious. She said, "Nobody asks straight people to do this. Why do we have to do this?" I told her that gay parents can and should set higher standards for managing family disputes. Look at how straight people are handling divorce and custody. Is that really the best we can do? That's incredibly disappointing. We have a responsibility to show that there's a better way.

Having an emotional network to support a family in crisis acknowledges that strictly legal protections rarely bring a comforting result when children are involved. Even when courts recognize a de facto parent's relationship, the children have still had to undergo the trauma of one parent challenging that status in the first place. "The case we have to make," says Firestone, "is that the ways in which straight people and probate courts handle child custody is inadequate."

By scrutinizing the inadequacies of traditional court systems, queer families have an opportunity to respond holistically to children's needs following a breakup. "People who care about a family and care about a child," says Firestone, "will look at issues beyond custody. Courts don't deal with the emotions and attitudes involved in cooperatively co-parenting a child in the wake of a divorce. These emotions and attitudes are what our kids live with every day."

Brian Anderson and his former partner, Ray, co-parent their son Mat, whom they adopted when he was five years old. When the fathers split up six years later, Brian moved out of the family home and now lives a mile down the street. There is no official custody agreement, but he sees his son almost every day, with flexible holiday and vacation schedules. Brian says they were able to spare Mat—a preadolescent at the time—from being involved in the painful details of their divorce by compartmentalizing issues:

> We sat down and told him what was going on, that his dad and I had reached this decision, that I was leaving, and that it wasn't his fault. We agreed that Mat was our number one priority. Mat is over *here*. What's going on with us is over *there*. Ray and I would meet away from Mat to talk and keep our issues separate. There was one time when Ray got very angry with me in front of Mat. Ray explained that he had been mad at me, not him, and apologized to Mat.

Because they live in a state that allowed both men to adopt their son, Ray and Brian are both listed on the birth certificate as legal parents. This legal status means that in the event of a custody struggle, both parents would have equal recognition. Any custody dispute would be determined on reasons other than legal loopholes. Fortunately, Brian and Ray are determined never to let it get to that point.

NEW BOYFRIENDS, GIRLFRIENDS, AND STEPPARENTS

Whether parents are emerging from a same-sex partnership or are coming out of a heterosexual marriage, the dynamics of dating, falling in love, and establishing long-term relationships are all more complicated when they have children from a previous relationship. Parents have additional decisions to make about their relationships, such as when to introduce a new love to the children, and what role that person will play in the children's lives.

A parent can never be too careful about merging his or her love life with family life. It might feel like a cozy idea to bring a new boyfriend or girlfriend into a ready-made family and fill the void that a separation has left in a household. For a parent who has recently come out, this impulse is even stronger if the new love is the main reason the parent came to terms with his or her sexuality. Waiting at least until the infatuation has subsided can help a parent see more clearly whether the relationship has staying power. Even if the relationship does grow to a point where the new partner is living with the kids and sharing parenting responsibilities, the children need to be reassured that the new partner is not a replacement for their other parent. Discipline can be an especially touchy issue. If the role of a new partner has not been discussed, children see the partner as infringing on parental territory, and resent it. ("She's trying to be my mom. She's not my mom!")

Not all children will like the individual their parent falls in love with, irrespective of gender. Some kids are determined to dislike a parent's new love interest before they have even met, only because they do not like the idea of their parent being in a new relationship. In families where a parent came out of a heterosexual marriage, it might be difficult to discern if children are having problems accepting the new partner because their mom or dad is now in a same-sex relationship, or because they simply do not get along with the individual. Parents are quick to assume that children's resistance to accepting a new partner is a homophobic response. For seven years Phillip's mother had a partner about whom Phillip felt conflicted:

> We had a love-hate relationship. She pissed me off because she was so controlling. But we hung out because we had a lot of common interests. Out of respect for my mom, I tried to get along with her. I'd get pissed because of the way she treated my mom, and then get pissed at myself for not telling my mom how I really felt.

If it really is difficult for a new partner and a child to get along, the child can feel like the parent is choosing the partner over the child. Some children tolerate the conflict; some choose to live with the other parent when they are old enough to insist upon it. I know of a handful of children whose conflicts with new partners reached such a boiling point that the children moved out and lived independently before they were legal adults.

Again, conflicts in families when parents are dating can arise in any family, regardless of sexual orientation. Children with parents from a mixed-orientation marriage will have many of the same issues in dealing with their straight parent dating again as they have with their gay parent dating again. One difference, however, is that when a straight parent is dating, marriage or an engagement gives children permission to officially recognize a stepparent as family. The transition from "Daddy's new boyfriend" to "Daddy's partner" or "my other daddy" is more nebulous.

In my family, I did not know when it was safe to invest emotionally in a relationship with Russ. I could not tell if this was a day-to-day deal, or if he was someone who would be sticking around. Dad and Russ were together over fifteen years before I learned they even had an anniversary date they celebrated. Although marriage was not an option, nor are they big fans of ceremony, my brother and I could have benefited from being part of an event that was meant to recognize our new family formation. Even something simple, like a family dinner, where the purpose was to discuss "us," would have helped. I needed to understand what role Russ was going to play in my life, and what obligations and responsibilities were going to be part of that relationship. Instead, our relationship was left unrecognized both outside of the household and within, and we had to make it up as we went along. It was a tentative, clumsy process that could have been made smoother with the help of an official milestone to mark the transition.

For other children, a gradual transition works well. Evan, 22, remembers when his mother was coming out because she was falling in love with her best friend:

> The relationship just slowly ebbed into a more significant status. It did this at a very normal pace; things just felt right on all sides. I did not immediately feel close to her daughters, but as I was an only child, I desperately wanted siblings. Regina [who is African-American] had been married to a Caucasian man previously, so her two daughters had mixed ethnic backgrounds. Oftentimes we get confusing stares from the waiters in restaurants when we all walk in together. They can never figure out who is with who and how many checks it will be. Over the years we have grown very close and refer to each other not as a stepfamily, but only as family.

Children who see their parents in new relationships have to make many adjustments. Some children find that a parent they always thought of as gay falls in love with someone of the opposite sex. The parent might officially come out as bisexual, or begin to identify as heterosexual, or not say anything at all.

After Sandy's mother left her marriage and came out as lesbian, she was with another woman until Sandy was about fourteen. At that point Sandy noticed an "odd dynamic" between her mother and a man her mother worked with doing door-to-door sales. Sandy remembers trying to make sense of her mother's blossoming relationship with her future husband. "I just knew it felt weird," says Sandy. "That was all very confusing to me, and even when they told me they were going to have a baby, I was not necessarily psyched about that at all. . . . When she was in [that marriage] she identified as [a] heterosexual mom and homemaker." It was not until that marriage ended that Sandy's mother began to use the word "bisexual" to describe herself.

Attraction to the opposite sex may be a new realization for parents, or something they had always known but had not seen the need to tell the children. Regardless, children of parents who were previously gay-identified may need some extra time to adjust to a parent getting involved in what appears to be a heterosexual relationship.

While dating, re-partnering, or marriage are high priorities for some newly single parents, others see dating as something too complicated to pursue while the children are young. Since co-parents Brian and Ray separated a few years ago, neither has re-partnered, nor has either made dating a priority. Brian comments:

Dating goes on the back burner until our son graduates from high school. It would take a very mature person to date either one of us and understand how closely our lives are intertwined. I still consider [Ray] my partner, just in a different

way. I have a real difficulty saying "ex." We really are so much
a part of each other's lives that "ex" just doesn't seem to work.

Co-parenting in a way that is the least disruptive to their son's life
means it is important that Brian and Ray continue to have contact
with each other. When a relationship without children ends, former
partners have the option of going their separate ways and starting over.
Having children, however, means that "exes" will always share a relationship of sorts, so it is in everyone's best interest to make the break
as amicable as possible.

When single parents start dating seriously, they often underestimate the strength of the bond between their children and the new
boyfriend or girlfriend and the emotional effect on the children if the
couple breaks up. Even when the ex is in the children's lives for a short
time, the ending of the relationship can be a profound loss for the
children—the equivalent of another divorce. In these circumstances,
however, the children are rarely assured that the ex-partner will maintain a relationship with them.

Tabby Dye, 20, felt abandoned when she lost contact with an ex-
partner of one of her mothers. Tabby's two mothers, Marla and Jean,
had already separated but still chose to adopt Tabby as co-parents. For
the first six years of her life, Tabby moved freely between their adja-
cent homes and Jean re-partnered with a woman Tabby called
"Nanna." When Tabby was six, Marla relocated and Jean assumed primary custody. At that same time, Jean and Nanna were breaking up.
Tabby's sadness over one of her mothers moving away was compounded by Nanna's departure. Tabby's relationship with her mother
Marla was consistently maintained despite the distance, but her relationship with Nanna—whose role had been vaguely defined from the
start—was completely lost shortly after Jean and Nanna broke up.
Tabby remembers:

When my Nanna left, I wanted to keep contact with her, but then things went sour between her and Jean. Jean tried everything to keep us apart, and it worked. At the age of six, when two people that you truly love move away for no real reason— or not for any reason that a six-year-old can understand—you tend to blame yourself. In my mind I was the common factor.

Parents might think that keeping an ex-boyfriend or ex-girlfriend in their children's lives would be too confusing, but if children have developed bonds with them, never seeing the ex again can be more confusing. When Samantha's dad was ultimately awarded custody after he and her mother divorced, Samantha grew attached to her father's partner, who was with her father until Samantha was eleven. When her father and his partner broke up, they continued to own a rental property together, where they both still live. During Samantha's teen years, her father's former partner was in an apartment down the hall, and today they still remain close. It was an arrangement for which Samantha is especially grateful in light of the emotional roller coaster she had already lived through when her mom and dad divorced:

> I remember [my dad and his partner] telling me [they were breaking up] and being very, very upset. It was so scary to imagine that this person who was in my life every day was suddenly going to go away. But it was also a smooth transition because he stayed part of my family. I really respect that their relationship ended, but in contrast with my mom and dad, it didn't have to destroy people's lives. They've never forgotten the value that they saw in each other in the first place.

Yes, Samantha's story is exceptional, but while it's true that ex-spouses do not have to live in the same building for the sake of the children, they can still support these connections in other ways. Whenever possible, children need the chance to say good-bye to a newly ex-boyfriend or girlfriend. Children should be allowed to stay in contact with them if they want to, whether it be through phone calls, cards, e-mails, or visits. One adult daughter remembers her mother's former partner picking her up for "specials"—their word for unofficial visitation when the two would go out for ice cream or another fun activity. As time passed, "specials" occurred less often and the relationship faded naturally, without the pain of a sudden break.

MAKING KIDS THE FIRST PRIORITY DURING AND AFTER DIVORCE

Successful co-parenting puts children *before* the divorce, rather than in the middle of it. It involves patience and a lot of communication. It means parents communicate with each other directly rather than expecting their children to be messengers. Even seemingly benign messages, such as "Tell your mom to call me about ordering your school pictures," can leave a child feeling stuck in the middle. Parents who truly can't speak civilly to each other should seek an alternative, such as a neutral adult mediator. Parents also need to avoid making disparaging remarks about their child's other parent, as Tabby comments:

> I want to tell the parents out there that if the relationship does not work out and you are sharing custody, get along in front of the children, and do not let them hear you fight. Do not talk bad about the other parent in front of the child. I hated [my mother] Jean for doing that my entire life. It will only push the child out of your life faster.

Negative comments overheard by children of divorce can lead them to believe that a parent disapproves of their love for the other parent. When both parents keep their feelings for each other separate from their children's love for them both, children will not have to choose loyalties or worry about hurting one parent by loving the other. Even when children side with one parent who could feel vindicated by their choice in the short term, the price for this loyalty might ultimately be too high. As years pass, children, once too young to understand, begin to piece family history together. After the children mature and are able to form their own opinions, the parent runs the risk of being resented by children who have come to feel that they were deliberately distanced from their other parent.

Successful co-parenting means minimizing the disruption in children's lives and staying flexible. Adjusting can be significantly less stressful for children if they do not have to transfer to another school or move out of their house. I have even heard from a few families in which the children stayed in the house and the *parents* traded homes every other week.

Because of visitation schedules, parents will sometimes miss being with their children on special occasions. It's understandable to feel sad about their absence, but there is no gain in sharing those feelings with the children. Parents who pout about not being with their children on holidays or birthdays only leave children feeling guilty when they catch themselves having a good time while knowing their other parent feels lonely. Another alternative, while unthinkable to some families, is to celebrate holidays together.

Joint custody and open communication are ideal, but sometimes one or both parents make that impossible. When an angry ex is acting out in particularly spiteful ways, it is tempting for the other parent to respond in kind. Young minds are malleable, and truths can be distorted to guide children into becoming sympathetic to one parent or another. During times when it is most tempting to respond aggressively to a former spouse's behavior, parents need to ask themselves how they hope their grown children will one day talk about the way their parents handled the breakup. No parent finds satisfaction in the idea that their grown children will relay childhood memories of endless court cases, bitter fights, visitation restrictions, or even total loss of contact with one of their parents. As any child who has been caught between feuding parents will tell you: even when one parent "wins," everyone has already lost too much.

By counting on supportive friends or counselors, parents will avoid getting their children involved unnecessarily with grown-up issues. When children sense a parent is not being cared for, they try to take on the responsibility of being the support system for that parent. Learning to cope with family changes with the help of an LGBT-friendly professional can do a lot toward smoothing the transition. It might work best for a parent to go to counseling alone or, if at all possible, with the other co-parent.

Now that I am grown, my own parents have become more relaxed about withholding their opinions about each other, and sometimes they let a negative comment or two slip out. It is still annoying to be put in a position of having to defend the other parent. The difference now is that I am old enough to form my own opinions rather than adopting theirs. I am free from the worry that one parent will use their power to limit my relationship with the other. As an adult, I choose what sort of relationships I will have with each of my parents, and I can assert myself when a parent is giving me information I do not want.

Making divorces "successful"—that is, minimizing the burden that falls on the children—is not easy. The extra patience and commitment parents put into a successful divorce are worthy investments. Parents who can co-parent well after a divorce assure their children that their family change does not have to leave a family "broken." As

Brian says about their two-household arrangement, "We still consider ourselves a family. We've been able to create our family, and now re-create our family. With the stereotypical families there are set rules. But we've been able to make up our own rules."

The decisions parents make in the midst of a breakup will affect children for years. Children should grow up to understand that these were the best decisions their parents could make at the time, and that they were choices that honored all the relationships involved. Regardless of the circumstances for the breakup, and regardless of what custody advantage one parent might have over another, both are the children's parents. When the task of parenting outlasts a partnership, it is important to keep the issues of the breakup separate from the issues of parenting. It is then that the children will feel safe and supported.

Four

Out into the World: Children of LGBT Parents in School and Beyond

I think the hardest part about this is that people tell me not to take people's comments personally. But I do. Every time. They are personal. This is my family.

—EMILY HANSEN, 23

At an LGBT community gathering, I caught up with a gay couple I had met seven years earlier when their two sons were toddlers. Back then, the couple had attended a panel discussion of teens that I moderated. When they pointed out their young sons, who were running around with a cluster of little ones, I mentioned that I hoped that as the kids grew older, their support networks would be even stronger.

"Oh, that won't be something our family needs," one of the fathers responded. "They have no problem with us being gay at all. They'll tell anybody, and it's just not a big deal for them. We're raising our children with pride."

This man's hope, which he shares with so many LGBT parents, was that if he and his partner simply provided their children with enough love, confidence, and self-esteem, the children would not feel they had to keep their family a secret. As young children grow up, however, their parents discover that beyond the pride they feel for their family, numerous other issues prevent children from always being open. While children integrate the love from their families into their lives, they are also bombarded by messages that say being gay is bad and that gay parents are unfit. They hear news reports about hate crimes and murders of LGBT people as well as political debates about the legitimacy of civil rights for LGBT families.

As I spoke with these two dads, they reminded me of our initial exchange seven years before. One of them said, "The first time I heard you talk, I thought, 'Not my kids!'" He took a step back from me and crossed his arms in front of his chest, an exaggerated imitation of his own denial. "But that was before they started going to school. We did not realize how much everything would change when we were no longer able to *control their environment*."

They went on to explain that their sons had become more selective about whom they tell about their family. Seven years earlier, the couple could not have imagined that their confident tykes who loved marching with them each year in the Pride parade would ever be anything but completely open about their two daddies. But one day, when they picked up one of their sons from camp, they learned that he had made up an elaborate story about his relationship with his fathers to get around revealing that his parents were gay. One of the dads said that the story his son made up made them realize, "That's what he needs to do right now to feel safe. Smart kid."

A smart kid with a couple of smart parents. Rather than feeling hurt or insulted, these dads did not assume that their son's cover-up was rooted in shame. They understood that their son's discretion was an age-appropriate response to homophobia and not a reflection of his feelings about his parents.

CHILDREN COME OUT, TOO

New LGBT parents often say that they thought they were as out as they could be—until they had children. Having children means that LGBT people are continually explaining their family to new teachers, doctors, day-care workers, religious leaders, and the parents of their children's friends. The ongoing coming-out process extends to the children as well. They also have to make daily choices about if and how to come out about their families to everyone around them, including friends, teachers, baby-sitters, Scout leaders, and coaches.

To some parents, the idea that their children have to "come out" seems absurd. They have avoided thinking about how society's reaction to their sexual orientation affects their children's lives. As I explained previously, sexual orientation should not be confused with sexual *behavior*. While the topic of sexual behavior is not regularly discussed among young children, the topic of *family* is. Already in preschool and kindergarten, children with LGBT parents are put on the spot. For example, a kindergarten teacher thinks nothing of having the children draw pictures of their families and share them with their classmates. When I knew I would be holding up my drawing to the entire class, I drew my mom and dad, but not my dad's partner. I was not ready to explain why my family picture had an extra man in it. For Derek, 33, this kind of class assignment was his first clue that his family was different. "I drew our family," he remembers. "Dad, my two brothers, me, Mom, and Donna. The teacher asked who Donna was. I told her 'Donna.' I thought every family had a Donna."

Some parents think that not talking about their sexual orientation with teachers and other adults in their children's lives will prevent drawing unnecessary attention to it. Unfortunately, their silence usually leaves children to conclude that their parents' sexuality is something shameful that they need to help their parents cover up.

Tina Fakhrid-Deen, 29, grew up with a lesbian mother. She followed her mother's example of silence:

> As a child, I don't recall ever admitting above a whisper that my mother was lesbian. I tried to act as if I didn't care. That was *her* business, right? The truth is that I was terrified to speak on that subject. People had been speculating for years and I'd outright deny it. What would they say about me if they found out? Would it make me as hated as folks seemed to hate homosexuals? I decided early on that it was probably safer to stay in the closet.

Grown children frequently say that their LGBT parents underestimated the effects and the pressures of navigating through a homophobic world. The issues that arise are not always blatant threats or harassment, but general ongoing discomfort about how people are going to react. Children may have a barrage of questions in their minds at any given time: *Will I be targeted if I challenge a joke that is homophobic? What will happen when my parents show up together at a school play, or a teacher-parent conference, or my soccer games? Should I say my mom's partner is her friend, her roommate, or her sister?* Many social interactions have the potential to raise questions from peers. If they are not well prepared, children can be caught off guard, confused about what to say, and worried that they will give the "wrong" answer.

Just because children are not talking to their parents about their different kind of family does not mean that they are not thinking about it—or worrying about it. They could already be dealing with it in their own way when their parents are not around to monitor the situation. Children may worry that if the wrong people find out, it could result in a parent getting fired. In other families, children fear that accidentally outing a parent might result in being shunned from their church or a parent's discharge from the military. Kids need permission to talk with their parents about these worries—whether they are real or perceived.

Each time someone considers coming out to someone new, there is a process—even if it lasts only a split second—of weighing the risks against the benefits. Since LGBT parents are adults, they have had years to experiment with making choices about coming out and dealing with other people's reactions. What no longer feels like a big deal to them can feel insurmountable to children who have not yet developed the skills or understanding to deflect ridicule and advocate for themselves. When children choose to remain silent about their families, it is rarely because they are ashamed, but because they want to protect themselves and their families from the unknown.

PREPARING CHILDREN FOR HOMOPHOBIA

There is a moment in every child's life when she learns that there is hate and pain in the world. Children with LGBT parents also become aware that some of that hate is directed toward their family, which threatens their sense of safety. Even the child who had no problem relating the details about his family to every baby-sitter, cashier, and telemarketer, might suddenly become withdrawn and hesitant as he gets older.

Darius Greenbacher, 32, recalls the point when he began to care about what other people thought:

> My mom was always out and every school year she made sure that she told all my teachers that I came from a lesbian family. I had very few problems or issues around my upbringing until puberty set in. From about eleven until maybe thirteen, it really scared me to have lesbian parents. I felt that if people

knew, they would think I was gay. Which now would have been fine, but at that time, there was so much pressure, so much homophobia, especially in those early years of puberty. And I was very, very scared and nervous about that. I grew up with a group of friends since kindergarten. We had sleep-overs at each other's houses and they knew that my mom and Judy had their own bedroom. Everyone just knew. But new friends I would make, I wasn't so open with them.

Like Darius, I was selective about whom I talked to, but for me it started at an earlier age. I cannot remember a time before adolescence when I did not feel like I had to be careful whom I told. I was aware that some people would hate my dad if they knew he was gay. He came out in 1978, a year after the "Save Our Children" campaign, which was spearheaded by gay-rights opponent Anita Bryant, a former beauty queen nationally recognized for her commercial endorsement of orange juice. Basing her argument on selective interpretations of the Bible, Bryant vehemently opposed a new civil rights ordinance in Florida's Dade County that banned housing and employment discrimination based on sexual orientation. Bryant claimed that because homosexuals cannot procreate, they need to "recruit" children. Her anti-gay message led to the successful overturn of the antidiscrimination ordinance in Dade County.

As a five-year-old, I overheard conversations about the "Save Our Children" campaign which I interpreted literally. I feared someone was going to find out my dad was gay and come to take me away to "save" me. I had no way of knowing who those people would be, so to be safe, I assumed it could be anyone at any time. (Although in my imagination the "bad guys" were always white men in three-piece suits.) I knew that sometimes people who were gay were attacked or killed. I could not figure out why some gay people became victims and others did not. In my mind, it was only a matter of time before my family was the next target.

Understandably, parents do not want their children living in fear of harassment or facing an onslaught of hurtful messages about their families. Today, more LGBT parents are taking deliberate steps to avoid exposing their children to such fears. These families have many more options to help them feel safe and affirmed than earlier generations. When it is financially practical, LGBT parents can choose to live in a gay-friendly neighborhood. If they are in a community where there are many LGBT families, they form play groups and see one another at regular events. Some families are even able to find schools where diverse families are welcomed and gay parents are commonplace. After a while, LGBT parents who are able to find a supportive environment can let themselves believe that the community they have built around them is representative of the rest of the world. They immerse themselves in gay communities where children have the freedom to live without knowing hate. It gets easier to deny that at some point their children will have to face the reality of homophobia.

Ashley Harness, 20, attended a very progressive school through eighth grade. Three of her teachers were openly gay, and some of her classmates had gay parents. Born through donor insemination to two mothers, Ashley began censoring how she talked about her family when she started ninth grade at a different school. Her self-censoring left her feeling stifled. In the eleventh grade she started a gay-straight alliance to help create an environment where she would not have to retreat to the closet. "I had no idea how free I was," Ashley says about her previous school.

Before they send their children off to school, parents should talk to them about what makes their family different, and how some people might criticize them for those differences. While it is sad to have to introduce this reality to children, it is preferable that they hear it from their parents first, in a supportive setting, before they encounter it on their own.

"My mom and Judy told me I was going to hear a lot of negative, hurtful things about gay and lesbian people," says Darius. "It was good to get that warning because I knew it was coming. It wasn't a shock. It wasn't like I was some happy-go-lucky little kid with two moms who [was stunned by] a bunch of homophobic nonsense."

It's a heart-wrenching choice for parents to make: holding off the sting of homophobia for as long as possible, or revealing the world's ugly side to help their kids develop coping skills early on.

Children's Confrontations with Homophobia

The concerns and anxieties of kids of LGBT parents change as they get older. In kindergarten, they are as basic as not wanting to hear mean things said about their parents. As years pass and children become more cognizant of sexuality, the fears are more about being rejected by peers, or being threatened or harassed.

Late-elementary and middle school can be particularly difficult as issues of sexuality emerge more clearly, and the meaning behind derogatory comments like "that's so gay" are finally understood. When children make the link between the insults and LGBT people, they begin to wonder if their classmates will react negatively to someone coming from an LGBT family.

Robyn, 27, was five when her father came out. She was perfectly comfortable with the relationship between him and his "roommate," but dealing with classmates was another matter:

My perspective changed when I finally figured out that the "gay" used in schoolyard slurs was actually referring to my dad. The understanding that the rest of the world was not necessarily accepting of my dad and my family came as a surprise. This did not cause me any shame, but a great deal of loneliness and sadness as I felt I couldn't be "out" about my family as a child.

Sarah Larkin, 20, also interpreted the slurs at school as a warning to be cautious. As a younger child, she had no hesitation speaking matter-of-factly to anyone ("the butcher or whoever") about "Daddy and Paul." By the time Sarah was in seventh grade—an age when "fag" and "that's so gay" are commonly heard at school—she realized that those derogatory terms were about people like her dad.

"I figured out that that was my father," Sarah explains. "He was a fag. He was gay. I understood that was not good. . . . I was really hurt. I loved my father and these kids were saying all these things about my father—not him necessarily—but it was *about* him. . . . So indirectly it was extremely hurtful; whether or not they said it to my face, it didn't matter."

At that point Sarah's father and Paul were no longer together. Without the presence of a partner, her father was not so obviously identifiable as gay, and Sarah saw no point in outing him. "To the outside world," she says, "he was just a single father."

Since anti-gay comments are typically about gay individuals, not their children, LGBT parents do not always understand that their kids internalize the hurtful words. Many parents find it hard to accept that children who are heterosexual or still undeclared would feel the sting of homophobia. It leaves parents asking their children, "Why would that bother *you?* It's not like *you're* gay."

Other parents dismiss the hurt too quickly by telling their kids to "just ignore" the teasing. Parents say things like, "I tell my kids if someone says or does something mean to them, it's not because there is something wrong with them. It's the bully's problem." While intellectually this is true, it does not make the pain go away. Parents need to deal with the hurt by acknowledging that although there is no truth to the teasing, it still might be painful to hear—and that it is all right to have these feelings. If parents do not validate a child's hurt feelings, they risk making the situation more stressful by leading the child to believe that if she is unable to "just ignore" it, her parents do not want to hear about it. This can lead to greater isolation for children, who might conclude that their feelings are unfounded.

Sarah says that not talking about the homophobia at school added to her anxiety. She wanted to bring it up, but because her dad had not talked specifically about being gay, she was not sure if she could:

A lot of my life would not have been so confusing and so painful if I had just been given the invitation to talk. Not cornered into anything, but on my own time. Because if I would have known that I could have gone to my dad when I heard teasing and told him, "It makes my stomach hurt when I hear it, and I can't stop thinking about it," I wouldn't have had to keep it to myself and I could have gotten rid of the stomachaches.

Arthur Elliott, 29, faced physical confrontations at school because people knew his mother was a lesbian. He remembers one incident in particular:

When I was walking across the lunch patio, there were a couple guys there and they were basically just rednecks and they followed me and knocked the books out of my hands. They knocked me down to the ground and said derogatory comments about my mom. Including that she had never had a "real man." That seems to be a popular comment. I've heard that all my life.

Amber Love, 25, who grew up in western Texas, faced ongoing harassment. She is lesbian, but since people perceived her as straight, the harassment was not because of her sexual orientation but because of her family. People in her town knew she had two moms, that her uncle had AIDS, and that her brother was gay:

> I encountered prejudice often. I experienced verbal taunts, was spat on by peers, had adults verbally harass me, children my own age and older threaten me with words, notes, and on a few occasions the threats escalated to me being backed up against a wall, grabbed, touched in a way that was uncomfortable. But I was never hit or sexually assaulted. I did not report what happened, especially when teachers were involved or had seen what happened and not intervened.

When students are able to find a supportive teacher who does intervene, there is the risk that the intervention will make a hostile situation worse. I once met a gay dad's fourteen-year-old daughter whose teacher stopped two classmates' taunts as soon as the girl asked for help. She did everything proud gay parents would want her to do: she did not closet her family, she refused to tolerate teasing, and she turned to an adult for help. Still, her self-advocacy came with a price. The students who were disciplined jumped her after school, calling her a "fag" and accusing her of "getting them into trouble." The fear of this sort of retaliation can prevent children from reporting harassment.

Even when the hostility turns physical, children do not always tell their parents. Children know that reporting such incidents can stir up a chorus of I-told-you-so's from judgmental people who maintain that it is "unfair" to children to be raised by LGBT parents. Children who want to continue to be supportive and loyal to their parents often keep harassment to themselves so their parents will not feel guilty or responsible. Many adult children admit to hiding their encounters with homophobia for the sake of their parents.

When I was a teenager, there was no way I was going to talk to my dad about how his being gay affected my life. In the seventh grade my friend's older brother found out that my brother and I slept in a fold-up double bed at our dad's house. Given the limited space in my father's home, I had not thought this strange, but my friend's brother convinced us that a gay dad's putting his son and daughter in the same bed was a secret that could destroy my family.

As "payment" for him not announcing our sleeping arrangements at his high school—where my brother was also a student—my friend was coerced into doing her brother's chores. It was a few weeks before he grew bored with this adolescent blackmail scheme. During that time, I was dreading the moment that he might create some drama at my family's expense just because he felt like it.

The best thing I could have done was something I refused to consider. I should have told my dad. But I thought, "If this is causing me so much anxiety and I'm not even gay, then how much will this hurt my dad?" I did not want him to feel that the mess I was in was his fault. What I did not understand was that because my father was an adult, he had more mature reasoning skills and was better able to deal with such a circumstance than I. He had years to become accustomed to homophobic mentalities, to work through, confront, or ignore them. If I had worried less about protecting him and been open about my problem, my father could have helped me diminish what was an all-consuming fear to more manageable proportions.

SHARED EXPERIENCES WITH QUEER YOUTH

Through research and their personal stories, queer youth report that hostile school environments have profound negative effects on them.

When confronted with homophobia, they sometimes resort to destructive coping strategies that include drug and alcohol abuse and truancy. Other adverse effects include low self-esteem, depression, and feelings of hopelessness, which are reflected in disproportionately high representation in statistics on attempted and completed suicide.[11] Research on the effects of homophobia in schools is typically specific to gay and lesbian youth and is conducted to build a case for why schools need to teach acceptance and respect for diversity. Since queer youth are suffering and are at risk of suicide, part of the solution is to help them feel safe at school.

The issues concerning youth and homophobia that have *not* been widely examined are how children of LGBT parents are affected by homo-hostile schools.[12] From a political perspective, revealing that these children face challenges similar to queer youth could serve to fuel the anti-gay position that LGBT people should not be allowed to raise children. Children of LGBT parents understand that the blame for peers' teasing or harassment could be unfairly placed upon their parents. Children who want to protect their parents often minimize the severity of hostile experiences in school so that they can uphold the "right" answer: that their parents' sexuality has no adverse effect on their everyday lives.

As in the case of queer youth, some children of LGBT parents who go to school in a hostile environment skip school, get poor grades, and struggle with depression and suicidal thoughts. Others cope with their emotions by using drugs or alcohol, or intentionally inflicting injury on themselves, sometimes referred to as "cutting."

Some sons and daughters "protect" themselves from harassment by engaging in risky sexual activity. They may feel pressured to "prove" that they are straight by having sexual intercourse earlier than many of their peers, and with numerous sexual partners of the opposite sex. Not only does being sexually active curb the questions about the child's sexuality, it also demonstrates to others that an LGBT parent was "successful" in creating heterosexual offspring. To such children, having sexual intercourse is perceived as an act of loyalty—a way to absolve their parents of suspected "recruiting."

For homo-hostile people who think that these risk factors should support restrictions on gay parenting, it is important to remember that the negative effects resulting from having LGBT parents are completely preventable. A mother of a thirteen-year-old knows that her former husband's sexuality is not the reason why their son is struggling. She explains:

> Billy's problems seem to be more . . . a result of public opinion . . . than [of] the fact that he has a gay father. Many other children are aware that he has a gay dad and they don't hesitate to throw this up in his face. Others just do the usual gay bashing, not directed at Billy personally, although he feels it deeply. Yesterday, on his way home from school, another seventh-grade boy followed him and accused him of being gay. He then proceeded in graphic detail to taunt Billy with sexual statements. My son arrived home devastated and did not want to return to school.

A parent's sexual orientation is not the problem here. The problem is socially supported and condoned homophobia. Most people who are in LGBT families understand the significance of this distinction.

While kids of LGBT parents share some parallel experiences with queer youth, their needs are not always the same. There are times when serving the two groups in the same ways works well, and other times when it causes conflicts. When I talk to teachers about supporting students who have LGBT parents, they often say systems for support are already in place, namely a support group for gay students that sons and daughters would be welcome to join. There are a number of scenarios in which this would not be appropriate.

If a parent recently came out, the student could be angry and make homophobic comments. It is unfair to expect queer youth to seek support only to have to listen to someone talk about how upset they are that a loved one came out to them. Conflicts between these two groups can happen for the opposite reason, too. Children of LGBT parents are often more queer-savvy than their peers, who are at the beginning of their coming-out process. This dynamic causes tension when queer teens are at a stage where they are suspicious of any classmate who is straight, so even the presence of children of LGBT parents feels threatening. Usually, when these tensions arise in a combined group, the kids of LGBT parents drop out because they grow weary of being suspect in a place where they are seeking support.

Activities that focus on advocacy, however, such as those sponsored by a gay-straight alliance, are opportunities for kids of LGBT parents, queer youth, and straight allies to all work together. Their common ground is that they want to get involved and confront homophobia. In such environments, their differences do not create the same conflicts that arise in support groups. When service providers are planning outreach to queer youth and children of LGBT parents, they need to determine if they will have a mixed group or separate groups based on the goals and structure of their meetings.

SCHOOLS SET THE TONE

For thirteen years children will be spending as much, if not more, time with their teachers and peers as with their parents. By virtue of the sheer amount of time children spend at school, the climate of acceptance or hostility is a primary influence on their feelings about their families and themselves. Many administrators and teachers do not see the need for making their school safe because they do not have evidence of violent gay bashing. They think it "isn't an issue" in their school.

Even if students are not direct targets of harassment, their ability to receive a quality education is in jeopardy if they don't feel safe at school. Some will skip school to avoid a run-in with a certain bully or a particular activity that makes them feel especially vulnerable. For example, "Opposite Sex Day" is a "school spirit" activity where students are encouraged to cross-dress, creating a situation rich with opportunities for homophobic and transphobic jokes. Children of LGBT parents also feel more vulnerable at school when gay-related current events gain national attention. Headlines about gay marriage or gays in the military, for example, incite anti-gay conversations around dinner tables of homo-hostile parents. Their children listen and then repeat their sentiments at school.

Incidents of threats and violence do occur in many schools, and of course they need to be addressed and prevented. Making schools safe, however, is not just a necessity for kids who have endured those extreme incidents, but also for kids who *worry* about becoming victims. Kids of LGBT parents do not need evidence of abuse to justify feeling unsafe in their schools. It is human nature for fears to become so overpowering that they exceed reality until those fears *become* our reality. For example, in October 2002, several states on the East Coast were paralyzed by three weeks of random sniper shootings. Schools shut down, outdoor activities were canceled, and people sprinted from their homes to their cars to avoid becoming a target. When the perpetrators were finally caught, communities returned to their normal routine. During all of this, no one questioned the precautions people had taken. Their chances of being the next target were less than one in a million, but the randomness of the crimes left people in the area asking, *Is today the day? Am I today's victim?* Eighteen people were shot during the sniper's spree, but millions more were terrorized.

The pervasive fear of being a random target mirrors the fear brought on by hate crimes. The unchecked presence of homophobia affects not only LGBT youth, but also sons and daughters of LGBT parents. I was never personally threatened or assaulted, nor was I ever verbally harassed in a way that couldn't be curbed early on. Knowing that there were other people who *did* have such stories was what frightened me. It was the *possibility* of people acting on their hate that left me asking myself every day: *Is today the day? Is today the day when the taunting starts? Is today the day I get beat up?* And without a policy in my school explicitly stating that such actions would not be tolerated, I wondered if teachers would intervene should those things actually occur.

Fear alone should be reason enough for administrators to care about creating safe schools. If children feel they are at risk for being singled out, teased, or physically attacked at any moment, paying attention to fight-or-flight cues takes first priority. It is hard to learn while functioning under the stress of a hypervigilant survival mode. Over time, consistent stress hormones can harm the brain's ability to store and process information.[13]

When I ask a child of LGBT parents "How's school?" we both know I'm not asking about academics. They tell me how kids treat them on the bus, which teachers have identified themselves as "safe staff," and which classmates they try to avoid on the playground. Kids in middle school and high school typically give an hour-by-hour rundown on the supportive or homophobic climate in each class. They are constantly assessing situations for homophobia, and figuring out where they need to be on their guard the most.

Similar to queer youth, children of LGBT parents keep their eyes out for hints that someone might be an ally to them—a friend or teacher they can trust. Teachers are especially important for helping students feel they are safe. They can validate the children's existence by incorporating books that feature LGBT families, and by incorporating prominent historical figures who happened to be gay into their lesson plans.

Even something that seems to be a small gesture, like displaying a "safe staff" sticker, can mean the world to gay-sensitive students, even if they never approach the teacher. Some teachers are more proactive in reaching out to specific students. Emily Hansen, 23, was thrilled when one of her teachers gave her an article from *Teaching Tolerance* magazine about a girl who had a gay dad. "I remember . . . how much that meant to me," says Emily. "It meant she supported me and was thinking about me. To this day, we are great friends. Now that I'm a teacher, we share many teaching ideas with each other. And I still have the magazine."

Teachers also help students feel safe and supported by not tolerating anti-gay comments in their classrooms and in the hallways. Homohostile teachers who do not confront the students who make these comments rationalize that to speak up would contradict their religious or moral values. They ignore anti-gay comments because they do not want to be perceived as defending homosexuality and therefore "condoning the lifestyle." Their silence, however, is not interpreted as neutral. Teachers who choose to look the other way when they hear a derogatory remark communicate to their students that expressing anti-gay sentiment is acceptable. Regardless of their personal views on homosexuality, all teachers need to speak up when they hear derogatory comments. If a homophobic climate that goes unchecked results in children skipping school, picking fights, or losing concentration, teachers have failed to help their students learn.

Some homophobic teachers find it perfectly acceptable to express their views to their students, as fifteen-year-old Korri explained in an e-mail:

> I think maybe five percent of my school, tops, is not homophobic. But I am not brave enough to tell them about my mom or to even ridicule them for making gay jokes. "Gay" is pretty much an insult word at my school and even teachers are not afraid to show their homophobic side. I had one

teacher once tell me that gay people *want* to be normal but cannot be. I wanted to shout, "They are normal," but I was too chicken. Everybody in the class pretty much agreed with her, which made me mad.

While some teachers overlook verbal harassment, students know that teachers cannot ignore fights. As a result, some children of LGBT parents become the instigators of fights believing it will bring attention to a conflict that needs mediation. A fifteen-year-old girl explains how she tried to stop the anti-gay language at her school:

I think homophobia progresses less and less once you get older, but it's still there, and in different ways. In high school, kids say "oh, that's so gay" and I don't think it even registers in their mind anymore what it means. "Gay" has just become this word for "stupid." And at a lot younger age, kids use "fag." I would get in fights over it at school. I would beat them up when they called me "fag" or when they called other people "fag." I got in a lot of trouble for that and it didn't solve the problem.

There are teachers who will not allow anti-gay remarks in their classroom, but sometimes the way they handle incidents in which such remarks are made sends a confusing message. If the put-down is stopped without discussion, kids might assume that their mistake was that they accused someone of being gay who was not. I remember when one of my teachers heard a boy call two other students "faggots." The teacher responded immediately by saying, "That's not appropriate!" But then he added, "They are *not* gay!" He might have meant well by not tolerating the use of the word, but his extra comment suggested that the slur is deserved by those who actually *are* gay.

Children feel safer when the school is consistent in its handling of these issues. They need to know that anti-gay epithets will be stopped every time. Children also benefit from attending a school that maintains an antiharassment policy that includes sexual orientation and gender identity. That way, school is a place where learning can be their first priority without constantly having to look over their shoulders.

Coming Out for Themselves

In an experience that parallels that of LGBT people, children coming out about their families carefully plan the first stages. One daughter in elementary school screened trustworthy friends by telling each one something that she referred to as a secret, but did not really care if other people knew. She waited a few days, and if her friends were able to keep the fake secret, she figured they could be trusted with the real secret about her dad.

Children's choices to be out or to be discreet about their family will change over time. Jon, 30, chose not to talk about his gay dad and lesbian mom, but in hindsight, it did not matter. "When I was growing up, I was very secretive about it," Jon remembers, "which ultimately turned out to be a complete joke. My perception was, 'Don't tell anybody, deflect the issue whenever possible.' But I realize now that everyone knew."

Like Jon, Adam, 25, also chose not to discuss his family with classmates. As someone who is biracial, Adam considered his mother's sexuality something that would make him different in yet another way:

I went to high school in an all-white, fairly conservative neighborhood. Overall, most of my peers would use "gay" as an insult. I probably even used it. There were no teens or families that I know of that were openly gay. They probably would have been put through hell. I think that on top of feeling not comfortable at school because I was new and in a less diverse environment, my mom being gay made me all the more un-comfortable. I never *once* thought about bringing this up to anyone in school. I probably would have rather died or some-thing before I would let someone at school find out.

In contrast, Arthur had no control over whom to come out to and when to come out because his family was so visible. When he began high school, his mother and her partner opened a feminist bookstore in their hometown in southern Mississippi, which "wasn't well received by other people." Sometimes Arthur worked at the store, and when classmates found out it was owned by his family, "people at school would give me crap." What was most surprising to Arthur was that some of the people who distanced themselves from him were longtime classmates, not just people who did not know him that well.

For the most part I was in the gifted classes with most of the same people in my classes over the years. So most of the peo-ple had known me, but they didn't know about my mom until they opened the bookstore. Most of the people were just fine about it. The people who weren't . . . it wasn't any-thing really overt. More like the cold-shoulder routine. There were a few snobby girls who were also really devout Christians—Baptists—who, when I walked into a room . . . would stop talking and stare at me. They had known me for years, but we didn't have the interaction that we had had be-fore. What did it matter to them?

It is the unpredictability of homophobic reactions that makes ex-periences like Arthur's so confusing. One unexpected negative reaction can change a child's mind about being open. It only takes one teacher, bus driver, or neighbor to flinch and say, "Your mom is *what?*" to make a child more cautious from that point forward.

When children with same-sex parents find themselves in situations where they "don't want to get into it," a common strategy is to talk about both parents interchangeably as if they were one person. For example, if a daughter of lesbians is talking about "my mom" in several different stories, she could be referring to one, two, or more mothers. Her peers, however, assume she has a single mother. This gets more complicated when children hang out at one another's houses. One twelve-year-old daughter told me that she invited friends over only when she was certain that only one mom would be home. It seemed like the easiest solution at the beginning of the school year, but she was growing anxious trying to keep track of which friend had been introduced to which mom.

Depending on children's feelings of safety and their stages in development, they make different choices about how to talk about their families, including when to keep quiet, to be out, or like Kirk Wisland, 30, to try a combination of strategies. Kirk was eleven when his father came out to him, and Kirk's first impulse was to tell a few people. "I didn't necessarily think I could trust them," he explains, "but I just needed to tell somebody." His openness resulted in a couple of people telling even less trustworthy people, which resulted in classmates directing jokes toward him. "[It was] not really harassment," he says, "[just] things that people thought were funny, that of course weren't funny to me."

The following year Kirk had the chance to make a fresh start at a new school. Since being open about his family had "backfired," when he entered seventh grade, he decided not to tell anyone that his father was gay. For Kirk, silence was a necessary strategy to get through junior high. He says:

I had to make a conscious decision that was very difficult. . . . Junior high was really tough for me, especially gym class and the boys' locker room. When young men start to develop sexual feelings, the last thing in the world they want to be is different. We wanted to outdo the other kids and make sure that you were the straightest guy in the room. In the early teens there's this group-think mentality and it's tough to figure out—probably even more so for guys. Especially at that age you don't really have the maturity to deal with those kinds of situations.

The habit of hiding can sometimes become so ingrained that children hardly notice the lengths to which they go to feel safe. A nineteen-year-old daughter of a lesbian mother told me that she couldn't understand why other kids of gay parents were so preoccupied with how to deal with issues in school. She had graduated from high school and never had a problem. I asked her how her teachers reacted when they met her mother, but she said her mother never came to school. When I asked how her friends reacted to her family when they came to her home, she said she never invited anyone over. Keeping school and home separate eliminated any opportunities for conflicts to arise in the first place.

Joe Hake, 22, was also intentional about structuring his life so that he would not have to be out about his family. He maintained his silence almost until graduation:

I isolated my social life to being just at school. I usually went home on the latest after-school activity bus. Outside of school I had no social life whatsoever because I didn't want anyone to know. My last year of high school I had this friend who I knew was pretty politically liberal. We went to the zoo and I told her there. She was like, "So?" After that I told everybody.

It was such a liberating experience. I can't even explain how
liberating that was. You know how people joke about the person who is obnoxiously gay [immediately after coming out],
and just has to tell everybody? That was me. I just wanted to
tell everybody.

When children find peers who are supportive, the peers sometimes
take on the responsibility of protecting their friend with LGBT parents. Because the friends know how much homophobia affects the
child, they try to minimize its impact, creating a phenomenon I call
the "buffer zone." They screen for homophobes who might be joining
their circle of friends, and they stop anti-gay jokes around them so the
child of LGBT parents does not carry the burden alone. The child herself might not even be aware of what her friends are doing. I first noticed my buffer zone in high school when two friends at a party were
appointed to distract me until a debate about the morality of homosexuality subsided in another room. It was weeks later that a friend
told me about what they made sure I did not hear that night. They
were right to assume it would have upset me.

The moment when a son or daughter is comfortable being fully
out about their family might occur in high school, but often occurs
after leaving home. When children are no longer living with their parents, they are free to take risks without feeling that they are putting
their family's well-being in jeopardy. As soon as I began college, I
would bring up the subject of my dad and his partner within the first
few minutes of meeting someone. Finally, it felt no different from how
everybody else talked about their families. The freedom that came
with the physical distance made me realize how afraid I had been
about "telling" on my dad and getting him in trouble. He had not told
me I should keep it to myself, but I did not want to be responsible for
something terrible happening to him if the wrong person found out.
Fifteen hundred miles away, there was no chance of that; he was safe.

Sons and daughters who have attended college commonly say it was an important turning point for them. On liberal campuses where differences are valued, students don't worry about how their peers will react about having queer parents. Sometimes the identity warrants extra respect. Darius enjoyed people's enthusiasm about his family in college. "I would actually get some credibility when I would tell friends," he says. "[I'd mention casually], 'Oh yeah, you know, I grew up in a lesbian household. Shoot, I've been in the Minneapolis gay and lesbian community since I was four years old. My mom used to take me to the women's coffeehouse.' And they'd be like, 'Boy, this guy is all right!'"

Tina's breakthrough also occurred in college, when her spontaneous coming-out surprised even herself. When she and her then boyfriend saw two men holding hands on campus, her boyfriend blurted out, "If I could just put them all in a hot-air balloon and blow it up, the world would be a better place!" Hearing his comment, Tina says "something deep inside me boiled over." She slapped him, and yelled, "Would my mother be on that hot-air balloon, too? She's gay also! Would she have to die for your stupid-ass cause, too?"

Tina's anger was not solely directed toward her boyfriend or his comment. She was reacting to years of enduring homophobia without saying anything about it:

> I slapped my ex for all of the years people told me that homosexuality was a sin. I slapped him for all of the secrecy and ignorance that envelops the black community about being gay. I slapped him for every child with a gay parent that lost their voice and [was] denied a part of their existence to "belong" to a hypocritical society. I yelled to release all of my [pent-up] anger, frustration, and confusion. I yelled because I love my mother. I was tired of being silent.

For children, coming out about their family is about *them,* not their parents. Part of their experience is learning for themselves about when to come out, when to stop a homophobic joke, and when to defend their families. When kids do come out about their families, it needs to be because they are ready to do so, not because they worry that their parents will feel betrayed or hurt if they do not.

LEARNING THE LESSONS FOR THEMSELVES

I was planning a party in high school and I asked Dad and Russ to put away the gay books and art so that I would not feel embarrassed when my friends came over. A number of people in my circle already knew about my family, but a few did not, including one boy I knew for sure was homophobic. When I talked about "straightening up" the house, my father asked why I would be friends with anyone who made me feel like I had to hide. I dismissed the question. The way I saw it, part of wanting my family life to be "no big deal" was not allowing Dad's sexuality to dictate my choice of friends.

Russ and Dad graciously put away the evidence. (Never mind that white carpeting, track lighting, and a grand piano remained!) They helped me host a fabulous party, which was one of the last times I went out of my way to hide my family. Seeing Dad and Russ go into the closet for me while catering to a known homophobe was too much. I began to understand for myself that if people could not accept my family, I probably did not want to be friends with them. My mom and dad had told me this many times before, but I was not ready to accept it until I came to the conclusion myself.

Parents and their children will often have different ideas about when to be out and when to be more discreet. It is an ongoing struggle to anticipate and adjust to these differences, especially since parents have full control over this issue for the first few years of their children's lives. When parents take children's discretion personally, they risk feeling hurt, offended, and out of control of their own identity. I once saw tensions rise at a panel presentation when teens talked about times when they wished their parents would be "less out." A father with younger children responded angrily: "I spent my whole life figuring out how to come out of the closet. Like hell my kids are going to force me back in!" He did not understand that to children, careful discretion about their parents is neither about identity nor about politics; it is about acceptance and safety.

Parents will not always understand the choices their children make about when they do or do not come out. Regardless, parents need to put their personal and political feelings aside to honor their children's coming-out experience, which in many ways is similar, though not identical, to theirs. Children need permission to ask for help when they want it, as well as permission to figure out some things on their own.

Five

Family-Defining Moments: Respecting Queer Families, from Grandma's House to the White House

I continued to think of Mom and Annette as a couple for the remainder of Annette's life. At times, I think I gave more weight to their relationship than they did.
—LES ADDISON, 35

"Sorry to put you on hold for so long," the airline ticket agent told me. I was scheduling a flight for Dad, Russ, and me to attend my uncle's funeral. The agent did not know if same-sex partners were included in the company's definition of family. If they were, Russ would qualify for the reduced bereavement fare. If not, his ticket would cost over a thousand dollars more.

"I had to find a supervisor who knew the policy on this," the agent explained. "We do consider your father's, um, partner to be a family member." Dad and Russ have been together for more than a quarter century, yet it is a stranger at an airline company who gets to decide if that relationship constitutes family.

I had dreaded making the call for fear of feeling the sting of homophobia that put yet another barrier in the way of my family getting treated like one. Even when an airline does have an inclusive bereavement fare policy, individual agents are not always familiar with it, so it takes some calling around. Justifying our relationships should be the last thing I have to do when a family member has just died. Hearing on my first attempt that yes, Russ is family, made me feel lucky. That's a big part of coming from a gay family—preparing for the barriers that invalidate my family, and feeling "lucky" on occasions when those barriers are removed.

It was one of countless "family-defining moments"—times when kinship is publicly named and acknowledged—that people without LGBT family members don't even have to think about. Family-defining moments may have insulting or affirming outcomes for a family with LGBT parents. These moments occur in public contexts, when laws or company policies are at issue. They also occur in more personal contexts, when, for example, neighbors or extended family acknowledge, or fail to acknowledge, same-sex relationships. The institutionalized homophobia of the legal system reinforces the culturally conditioned homophobia of social situations, and vice versa.

Despite parents' efforts to raise children in strong and safe homes, the validity of LGBT families is questioned every day by broader society. When families are slighted, children frequently take it more personally than do their parents.

In big and small ways, children of LGBT parents face discrimination against their families that affects them legally, financially, and emotionally. Because non-LGBT families don't have reason to pay attention to homophobia, they rarely understand the adverse effects on children of LGBT parents until these inequalities are brought to light.

STRAIGHT FAMILY PRIVILEGE

Most families with heterosexual parents would not think to describe themselves as a straight family, nor would they be able to give examples of the privileges this status affords them. Privilege held by a dominant group is rarely noticed unless it is pointed out. My conception of straight family privilege is based loosely on what writer and researcher Peggy McIntosh calls "white privilege." McIntosh, who is white, examined the privilege that comes with her skin color. She outlined some of the daily details white people overlook in a racist society where white is considered the "norm." As examples, she explains that she can behave badly or appear unkempt in public without it being a poor reflection on her race. She can walk into a meeting confident that she will not be the only white person in the room, and knowing she will not be expected to speak on behalf of all white people.[14]

As a result of white privilege, white people are the last to notice institutionalized racism. When systems exclude and discriminate against people of color, racism assumes they will make compromises or just put up with it. McIntosh acknowledges the parallels between white privilege and male privilege and heterosexual privilege, but warns against labeling various kinds of oppression as "the same." She writes, "One factor seems clear about all of the interlocking oppressions. They take both active forms which we can see and embedded forms which as a member of the dominant group one is taught not to see."[15] Looking at privilege in this context helped me see that heterosexual families are typically unaware of the ways our society assigns them reverence and respect.

As an African-American daughter of a lesbian, Tina Fakhrid-Deen, 29, recognizes the similarities between institutionalized racism and institutionalized homophobia in her life. Both are constantly present, yet invisible to people who have been granted the privilege not to notice:

I feel like being in an LGBT family is very similar to being black. I'm accused of being overly sensitive to racism and homophobia. They think I am looking for it, but I'm not. Every day there are things said or done that you know are racist or homophobic, but they happen so much that it's hard to come up with specific examples right on the spot. I just know it's everywhere. But for white people and heterosexual people, it's not their experience, so it's not even on their radar screen.

Ashley Harness, 20, found the concept of straight family privilege applicable to her experience of growing up with lesbian mothers. At her college, she incorporated examples into a diversity training exercise about heterosexual privilege. After leading the exercise for the first time, Ashley found that even though her gay friends were acutely aware of the effects of homophobia on their lives, they did not recognize the privilege they were automatically granted as children of heterosexual parents:

> My queer friends are astonished at the heterosexual privilege my exercise grants them. "But I'm gay. . . . I don't have heterosexual privilege," they claim. "But you *do*," I think. "You do because you grew up in families with heterosexual privilege. You can talk about your family of origin with the same ease straight people talk about their families, without giving it a second thought." That's heterosexual privilege of which I cannot partake.

A child from a straight family can see other straight families on television without hearing them described as "controversial." A heterosexual parent who is receiving health-care benefits through work can add a spouse and children to the plan without having the coverage taxed as income. A child with straight parents can fill out school forms that have blank spaces for "mother" and "father" to accurately reflect her family structure. Children in straight families can seek help for emotional or academic problems without service providers wondering if their parents' sexuality is at the root of the difficulties. These are just a few examples of how straight family privilege provides children of married heterosexual parents with social access and affirmation on a daily basis.

FAMILIES NAVIGATING THEIR WAY THROUGH INSTITUTIONALIZED HOMOPHOBIA

Contrary to a common perception that anti-gay laws affect only LGBT people themselves, homophobia affects entire families. Laws that limit the rights of LGBT people also affect the rights, as well as the self-esteem, of the people around them who love them—especially their children. The lack of so-called special rights which prevent discrimination on the basis of sexual orientation or gender identity makes LGBT people vulnerable, therefore making their dependents vulnerable.

For example, a lesbian mother who has been working at the same company for several years could be transferred to a new department that is overseen by a homophobic manager. Despite the employee's history of outstanding performance reviews, her new boss finds out she is lesbian and fires her, leaving her struggling to support her family. Most people would think it unfair to fire employees just because they are gay, yet such discrimination is allowed in the majority of states.[16]

The effects of homophobia on a family are felt not only in the area of employment, but also in other situations that discriminate against gay people, such as the Boy Scouts. The organization does not allow gay men in leadership roles, which means a gay father cannot volunteer to lead his son's troop. Proponents of this regulation argue that it does not discriminate against boys in the program, since it applies only to adults. Technically this is true; a gay dad's son is still "welcome" to stay in the troop. It is next to impossible, however, for a child to feel comfortable in an organization that has labeled his father as a pariah.

When discrimination like this occurs, it reinforces broader society's view of LGBT people as less than worthy. This is a confusing and upsetting message for their children to process. Homo-hostile legislators and voters argue against laws that protect the rights of LGBT people, dismissing such laws as "special rights." Homo-hesitant people—those who have no connections to the community—are led to believe that passing nondiscrimination laws will give LGBT people preferential treatment.

What are labeled as special rights are not special at all; they are human rights that are currently being denied to LGBT citizens. The argument that gay rights are special is convincing to straight families who do not see the privilege they have. When they hear the word "special," many truly believe LGBT people are pushing to gain extra rights which will infringe upon their own. LGBT families and supporters need to educate this group of citizens about the rights to which LGBT citizens are currently denied access. Navigating through systems that fail to recognize the rights of LGBT families is insulting, tedious, and at times, frightening.

Shortly after I graduated from college, my father was out of town when Russ suffered a stroke and was hospitalized. After Russ's houseguests told me what had happened, I called the hospital and was directed to a nurse. When I asked for information about his status, I was asked if I was his wife. I had never had to deal with hospitals before, but I had heard horror stories about gay families not having access to their loved ones. I told her I was his daughter and I was forwarded to another line. This time I got the details I needed and was not asked to disclose anything about my relationship to him. When I arrived at the hospital, no nurse or doctor stopped me as I headed to Russ's room. I got to his bed and he was fully conscious, upright, and able to talk. Only then did I let myself relax. I had anticipated that at some point I was going to have to defend my right to see Russ. I felt like I had just walked down a hallway strewn with land mines, none of which, luckily, had gone off.

Again, I felt *lucky* that no one had stopped me from seeing my father's partner. I felt *lucky* that in a time of a family emergency I was able to do what straight families take for granted.

Living in a world of straight family privilege means having to be prepared at any moment to advocate for your family. Les Addison, 35, faced many of these challenges a few years ago when her mother's partner, Annette, was dying of cancer. While straight families in a crisis like this can focus entirely on the needs of their loved one, Les's family had to worry about how doctors, bosses, coworkers, caregivers, and extended family were going to treat their family.

Flying from San Francisco to Louisiana, Les arrived at the hospital to find out that her mother and Annette had identified themselves as sisters, and Les had been "demoted" to the status of niece. Like many LGBT families in need of medical care, the mere potential of hostility or discrimination was enough to prevent them from coming out at the hospital. "In the stress of the situation," Les says, "I was not feeling particularly glib. I had variously referred to the patient as my mother, my stepmother, and now, my aunt. It was very difficult to be in this emotionally trying time and feel like I needed to worry about slipping up and using the wrong term."

How the hospital workers would have reacted to the truth was unknown, but the middle of a family crisis is not a propitious moment for an LGBT family to risk finding this out. Les wanted her parents' relationship to be recognized, but at the same time she wanted to respect their choice not to disclose the truth. Les decided it would be safe at least to tell the supervising nurse of the home health-care providers. The nurse drove a pickup truck that sported a rainbow bumper sticker, a signal to Les that she was also gay. "'I just want you to know, my mother and her partner are not sisters,'" Les reported telling the nurse.

"Her response was a blank look for almost a minute while she tried to figure out what I meant. It helped me to know that there was someone who knew what was going on."

Both women had a medical power of attorney, so Les's mom had the legal right to visit her partner in the hospital and make medical decisions. What they were most concerned about, however, was being confronted by any one person's homophobia in a time of crisis. Despite having the proper paperwork, Les says, "they felt that both access and medical care might have been compromised if they had been out."

When Annette died, Les had no problem getting her paid bereavement leave approved because her employer already knew and respected her family structure. Technically, however, Les's relationship to Annette was not covered in the bereavement policy. Plenty of LGBT family members do not have employers who are as flexible as Les's—another employment benefit that straight families take for granted.

As Les handled numerous end-of-life issues, she also faced the challenge of interacting with extended family, which Les describes as "a large, religious blue-collar family, most of whom stayed in their hometown." While some of Annette's family members were very understanding of Les's relationship to Annette, others were "totally clueless and offensively close-minded." She was in contact with a number of them while she was coordinating in-house hospice services during the last several weeks of Annette's life:

> During the course of that, I had frequent phone and e-mail contact with her extended family. [I] was pleasantly surprised by how loved and appreciated I was by a number of her family members. I was also tremendously insulted by the one great-niece who thanked me for being there—as though I was doing a favor to the extended family. She wasn't recognizing that I

was there to take care of the woman who had been my mom for thirty years.

It was a time when it was most important for Les's relationship with Annette to be honored and acknowledged. Most of Annette's extended family, however, still didn't understand.

The advantage that Les had over many other children of LGBT parents was that she was an adult and therefore better prepared to advocate on behalf of her family. Younger children in similar crises will need someone to advocate on their behalf, such as a close family friend or neighbor. That person needs to know what barriers the family might encounter, and have access to all necessary documents.

FAMILY OUTINGS

Many important family-defining moments are not determined in a hospital or at work, but in a more personal setting—like the living room. When kids go with their LGBT parents to visit grandparents and other extended-family members, they often watch their parents take on a personality that is unfamiliar to them. Their parents revert to the role they played growing up, which involves being pseudo-closeted. This transition might be so ingrained that the gay parent does not notice he is doing it; but it can be jarring for his children. They are not sure if they, too, are expected to take a step into the family closet.

While many LGBT people are accustomed to not being "openly gay" when they visit their parents, their children can be less willing to make this accommodation. They know what their parents are like in more open settings and resent that they are pressured to maintain different personas in order to be accepted by family. It is common that the children are bothered by family dynamics that their parents have learned to ignore. For example, while a lesbian mother might agree to visit her own parents at Thanksgiving without her partner, her children are outwardly angry about the exclusion. They are the ones—not their mom—who threaten to stay home if their mom's partner is not included.

When extended-family members do not acknowledge or validate LGBT family relationships, it hurts the children as well as their parents. Except when extended-family members are extremely homophobic, relatives' inability to validate same-sex relationships within their family is generally not meant to be hurtful. More often they lack the understanding, words, or permission to affirm the family the way the LGBT family wants to be affirmed. Adding to the complications is that some same-sex couples are not sure of how they want their relationships recognized, especially in public settings. Individual members within a family are known to have differing ideas about how they want their relationships presented.

When Tina was getting married, she was excited to know that her mother was going to attend with her partner of two years. Tina and her husband planned a ceremony small enough for everyone to introduce themselves. Tina saw this as an opportunity for her mother to come out about being in a lesbian relationship, and was disappointed when she did not:

> When it was my mother's turn to stand, she said her and her partner's name and, without blinking an eye, introduced Kelly merely as a "friend" of the bride. What? All of the years spent with me calling her partners "aunt so-and-so" were supposed to be shattered [so that] truth and acceptance [could] step in at this very moment. They had just purchased a home together, donned shiny new bands on their ring fingers, and were supposedly deeply in love. She wasn't just a friend of the bride, she was my mother's *wife*.

Tina saw her mother's choice not to officially come out as a missed opportunity to honor her relationship in the same space where her daughter's marriage was being celebrated. Tina wanted her mother's public declaration to "break the traditional wedding mold." She later understood that while a more public recognition of her mother's relationship was important to her, her mother didn't necessarily feel this way:

> What I realized was that even on my wedding day, I was fighting for a cause. I was fighting for my mother to feel accepted and to help other family members see that her love was worthy of being honored. But the problem was, it was my cause, not theirs. Now I know that this choice to be visible has to be their own, and for now, just the fact that they are together is declaration enough for them.

Weddings—as events that are steeped in traditional family and gender roles—bring up many concerns for straight children of LGBT parents. Some children deliberately choose to have small weddings to avoid gambling with rude reactions from distant relatives or coworkers. Most of the anxiety is about how family and guests will react to the bride and groom's decisions about how parents and their partners are acknowledged. Who, if anyone, will walk the bride down the aisle? How will parents' partners be named on the invitation or in the program? How will the guests on the groom's side react when they find out the bride's father is now a woman? Which father of the bride gets the first dance?

Most family members have unspoken expectations about how these details should be handled. LGBT parents who are preparing for a child's wedding should talk to the engaged couple ahead of time so that no one feels hurt or put on the spot at the ceremony and reception.

The defining moments in my family have revealed themselves not at weddings but at funerals. The discomfort my extended family felt about my dad being gay was something we all tried to ignore on a day-to-day basis. But when my grandfather died quite suddenly, it was impossible to ignore. From what my father told me, I understood that after my father came out to his parents, they told him they loved him. My grandfather told Russ he was welcome in their home anytime. Afterward, however, little was said about my dad being gay, and Russ joined us on less than half of our trips to see our grandparents.

The silence around this issue when I visited my grandparents was in stark contrast to the open invitation I had to talk to my own parents. I thought my grandparents, aunts, and uncles preferred not to talk about it, so I went out of my way to avoid conversations that might remind them that my family was different. As time passed, each member in my extended family made unfair assumptions about everyone else. We each assumed that it was everyone *else* who didn't want to talk about this, so none of us did. And that silence came to be interpreted as shame. That silence was perpetuated through the years, and the cost of trying to make everyone comfortable with the situation led to a lot of awkwardness and discomfort. Conversations about my father's coming-out should have been revisited regularly, especially when new cousins were born. Instead, the younger children grew up in the silence. One of my cousins was fifteen before she asked her father if her uncle was gay.

When my dad's father died, in the midst of funeral arrangements, taking care of Grandma, and going through emotions of shock and grief, there was another issue that had to be addressed: What were they going to do about Russ? My uncle worried about how the family would explain who he was at the viewing and where he would sit at the service.

I wanted to yell, "Why couldn't he be there as Lee's partner?" Weeks later Grandma told my father that he "had to have understood" why his relationship with his partner had been nullified for the weekend of the funeral. She said the concern was that if the town found out Lee had a male partner, all of the attention that was given to the funeral would have been diverted to my father's sexuality. It wasn't the time to bring it up, Grandma reasoned. She was right. A funeral is not the best time for a coming-out party. However, my dad had come out more than twenty years earlier. That is plenty of time to gently share the news with neighbors.

Russ rose above the tension and attended Grandpa's funeral, lingering respectfully in the background. His name was not included in the list of surviving family in the obituary. My father said nothing, but I was incensed. I talked to an aunt and uncle about the omission as calmly as I could, not wanting to add to the drama. I pointed out how Dad's siblings were named with their spouses, but Dad was listed without Russ. My aunt and uncle justified the omission by saying that "not everyone's" spouses were included, since the spouses of grandchildren were not named. This was not a fair parallel, since my father was not a grandchild; he was the firstborn son.

Two months later my father returned to his hometown to attend his forty-year high school reunion. He learned that several of his classmates already knew he was gay and now he thinks it was more common knowledge in his hometown than his family wanted to believe. My father's family put years of energy into hiding a secret that really wasn't much of a secret. And for what gain? The only thing it did was offend and alienate family members.

The way my immediate family was treated at my grandfather's funeral was not intentionally disrespectful. But it was painful. Looking back, I see what we could have done differently to prevent this misunderstanding: We could have *talked* about Dad being gay and how that affects our family. And we could have given other family members permission to mention Russ to others, and helped them figure out what words they were comfortable using.

Unless it's explained, extended family members who are heterosexual do not recognize the privileges their LGBT loved ones are denied. This needs to be pointed out to them. That way, they would understand how insensitive it was to expect my father to pass as a single heterosexual at a time when he needed his partner most. If we had talked about it, they could have seen how much it hurt me when they did not acknowledge this man who had been in my life for more than twenty years, despite my lack of words to describe our kinship. But from their limited experiences with gay issues, they thought they were doing us a favor by not outing my family to their town of one thousand residents. Without us telling them, they really had no way of knowing any appropriate alternatives to kicking us back into the closet.

My younger cousins, taking their cue from the silence, consider their uncle's gayness to be a secret that must be kept. One of my cousins was in her high school civics class, where the "My Turn" column I wrote in *Newsweek* about my family was read and discussed. She and I have different last names, so during the class discussion she did not mention that we are cousins. She only said she knew me, but after a few classmates gasped she changed her story and said that she didn't really know me; her mother knew my parents. My cousin was not being intentionally hurtful by denying that we were related. I know this because she told me the story herself without a hint of remorse. From what she had observed around her, the only appropriate thing to do was keep quiet.

Communicating with extended-family members about LGBT relationships is not an instant solution. It doesn't mean that simply by talking about it everything will go perfectly smoothly from that point forward. But at least it would clarify how people really feel, instead of making assumptions. There will be times when family members make mistakes, but the sooner these can be acknowledged, the sooner everyone can move on. When I pointed out the omission of Dad's partner's name in the obituary, I would have been fine had someone said, "Gosh, we didn't even think of that. We should have asked your dad about that before we did it." Instead I got some unimpressive explanation that only left me feeling more alienated than before.

There is the possibility that some family members are truly homophobic rather than just oblivious. Non-supportive family members don't see that their exclusion of an LGBT parent hurts children deeply. Sean, 27, remembers the conflict that erupted in his father's family when his father came out as transgender, "almost to the point that they had disowned him." Sean and his sister were caught in the middle when the holidays came around and their uncle invited them to a family gathering:

> He explicitly stated that we would be invited but Dad wouldn't be. He likes to pretend that he speaks for the whole family. In reality, he doesn't necessarily speak for everyone, but that was the implication that was made. It really bothered me . . . [my uncle] put me on the spot at that point; it felt like we had to make a choice . . . we thought that was bullshit. By [accepting his invitation] we would be turning our back on my dad. That would be really cruel.

His uncle seemed oblivious to the insult to Sean and his sister implicit in his bigoted rationale for excluding their dad. Sean's uncle explained that the family needed to "protect the children." Sean says, "The impression was that my dad's presence would confuse the kids in the family. I wanted to be like, 'Um, Heather and I were raised by Dad.'"

As much as a family member might say the exclusion of the LGBT relative is *just* about the parent, to the child, it is never *just* about the parent. Even as adults, children see the rejection of their parent as a rejection of them, too. For Sean's uncle to suggest that Sean's father's presence was potentially harmful to children brings into question what their uncle thinks about how Sean and his sister were raised.

While Sean says his father's family is coming around slowly, some children of LGBT parents find the tensions between their parents and extended families to be too much to overlook, causing them to distance themselves. Many sons and daughters have little to say when asked about relationships with extended family because they simply do not interact with them. To be estranged from extended-family members is not a decision they make lightly, and many are ambivalent about the loss of these biological ties. Indeed, in queer culture, "family of choice" is often valued as much as, if not more than, family of origin. It is not uncommon for children of LGBT parents to base primary social networks on connections other than blood relationships. When an LGBT person is not accepted by their family of origin, choosing to no longer consider non-supportive relatives as "family" can be necessary for emotional well-being. Sometimes their children make similar choices.

Danny Crosby, 31, whose father was mostly closeted up to his death, holds his family partly responsible for the difficulties in his father's life:

> I no longer have anything to do with my father's family. That is my choice though. I miss certain members of his family: uncles and aunties, cousins. I do not want anything to do with either his mother or sister, though. I have too much anger toward them. This has to do with the lies and deceit that they fostered. They encouraged him to cover up who he was.

David Wells, 28, says that while his mother's parents didn't speak often about David's gay father, the negative things they did say made an impression. "There were phrases like, 'We like your dad but he does things that we don't approve of,'" recalls David. "Never blatantly judgmental, even though they were definitely prejudiced people. But they did get their point across about how they felt about my dad."

Mike Beebe, 33, says being open about his family has been necessary in order to get other people to understand how he expects his father to be treated:

> I think that has a lot to do with the fact that I am so proud
> and accepting of my father that I don't give people the space
> or the permission around me to be discriminatory. I know in
> plenty of families there isn't control over those circumstances.
> I do think I carry myself in the world in a way that demands
> respect . . . so therefore I hear fewer discriminatory comments.
> [I say,] "You know my dad is gay . . . do you have a problem
> with that?" So I think my prepping cuts off the opportunity for
> discrimination as well.

Being officially out as a family before the time of a crisis or a celebration is an emotional insurance plan. It's the security in knowing a family can come together when they most need one another and no one's sexuality will be a secret or a distraction.

How Language Fails Us

Even if we want to talk openly about our family relationships, finding the right kinship terms is a challenge. As language is often dictated by the culture in power, heterosexism limits the words we have to describe queer relationships. Kinship terms are sometimes more important to the relatives of LGBT people than to the LGBT people themselves. For example, my father never told me that Russ was his . . . anything. It had not occurred to him. Russ was simply "Russ." My father knew what their relationship was, so what else mattered? What mattered was that I needed a word. "Stepfather" implied he was married to my mother. "Other father" raised too many eyebrows.

"Uncle" felt too distant, so I stuck with "Russ." Years later I decided to refer to him as "my father's partner," but that term is less than ideal.

A few days before my college graduation, I brought my family to the campus library to show them where I had been earning my work-study dollars for the past four years. I stopped by the circulation desk to pick up my final check. A coworker commented on my cute two-year-old nephew running around and then asked about the rest of the crowd. I pointed out my sister-in-law first and then identified the others, two men and a woman, as my parents. "But which one is your father?" I'd had a feeling she would want specifics. I pointed as I said, "That's my dad, and that's his partner."

"His *partner?*" she exclaimed. I held my breath. "Well," she continued, "isn't it wonderful that your father's partner came across country with him to see you graduate!" I exhaled, appreciating that she got it and that she thought it was wonderful. But then she added, "What kind of business are they in?"

I often confuse people when I talk about my family because our language leaves me unable to clearly convey our kinship as straight families are able to do. LGBT families often lack appropriate nouns, which results in the need for something close to a short paragraph to explain our relationship with each family member. For example, the daughter of a lesbian mother who has a partner who also has a daughter can only refer to that other child as "my mom's partner's daughter." (Straight families can say "stepsisters.") I have heard people experiment with expressions like "sort-of-my-stepsister" and "kind-of-my-mom" but having to put a devaluing expression like "kind of" or "sort of" before something as important as family rarely sits right. Mike still spends time with the son of his dad's former partner, but can't quite find a way to describe their relationship:

I finally decided to call my father's partner's son "stepbrother" and then my father and his partner broke up or "divorced." So now I hang out with my "stepbrother" from time to time and really don't have language for who he is now. Is he my "ex–kind-of-stepbrother" or do I go into some kind of long-winded explanation. . . . I am pretty adamant about being "out" about my family, but sometimes it's just too many words.

Not having the names for relationships makes it difficult to convey their importance outside of the immediate family. Within the family, kinship terms are less important. For example, lesbian couples who have a baby together often want the child to call each parent a variation on the word "mother." As children in these families grow up, however, it's not uncommon for them to refer to both mothers by their first names for the sake of clarity when people don't understand the subtle yet important distinction between "Mama" and "Mommy." Outsiders may find it distant and impersonal when they hear a child referring to parents by their first names. But if this is what works best for the children, it doesn't diminish the relationship between them and either of their mothers.

Selecting a kinship term for a sperm donor is also complicated and often emotionally charged. If the donor is not an active co-parent, mothers usually want to avoid referring to the donor as "Dad" because the word assumes he has a relationship with the child that is as important as the two moms. Again, many children work this issue out themselves, although sometimes the mothers are uncomfortable with a child's word choice. Children sometimes find it easiest to explain their families by referring to a donor as the "biological father" or simply their father—even if they have no emotional connection to the donor.

Jesse Gilbert, 30, says that having words to describe his family was not important to him until he started going to school. It was there that he was expected to talk about his family. "That was one of the biggest

issues when I was a child," Jesse explains. "How do I name these people? How do I present these people to the rest of the world? What
should I say?" The lack of kinship terms was also problematic when his
friends' parents asked about his family. "I tried things like 'guardian,'
but nothing worked very well. I just call them 'my parents.' That's
what they are. There definitely has to be some language expansion."

Language continues to be a challenge for families, something we are
all making up as we go along. Currently many families are utilizing variations of heterosexual terms, such as a gay man calling his partner his
"husband," or a mother calling her gay son's partner her "son-in-law." In
years to come, borrowing heterosexual kinship terms will not be the
only option for LGBT families. As more families examine the limitations of language, new kinship terms will emerge for queer families—
terms that are both technically and emotionally accurate.

A few years back Russ introduced me to one of his colleagues at a
party by saying, "Abigail's father is my partner." The man squinted at
me and tilted his head. He didn't get it. Russ sighed, put his arm
around me, and told him, "It's complicated." I could not help but clarify: "No, it's not complicated. There's just not a word for it."

We need a verbal revolution.

HELPING FAMILY MEMBERS BECOME ALLIES

If family members learn how to advocate for their own LGBT family
members, they begin to feel more comfortable in advocating for LGBT
families in general. They can become passionate and articulate allies if
they know they are welcome to participate by talking about their own
families.

A same-sex couple might feel silly pointing out the obvious
("we're gay"), but without the official acknowledgment, family members might not know they are *supposed* to know. They might fear that

asking questions to LGBT relatives will make them uncomfortable, and that talking openly about it to others is an invasion of privacy. This is particularly true for relatives who see being gay as only "what you do in bed." If a straight father thinks that sexual behavior is all there is to being gay, then to mention that his son is gay at his bridge club would feel equivalent to discussing the son's sex life. If relatives don't think they can tell their friends about a gay family member, they are certainly not going to feel comfortable contacting their legislators about policies that will affect LGBT families.

I was twenty-seven the first time I heard my grandma say the word "gay." It was during a conversation prompted by the publication of my first column about LGBT families. Without talking specifically about my own family, I was able to talk about why I was writing the column and why it was important to me. Within a few moments, the woman who had only dared to go as far as saying "like that" in the past two decades was now saying "gay and lesbian." She had been given permission to talk and also knew what words she could use. That's not to say she went back to her town and founded a PFLAG chapter, but for Grandma, this was a huge first step.

Family members can take their first steps to becoming allies when they know it's okay to ask questions. Some of the questions might seem ignorant or difficult to deal with, but if they want answers, it is best to get them directly from an LGBT person or ally. What they ask could be very revealing about who or what else is influencing their perception about LGBT issues. The questions might be surprisingly basic, or they might reveal naive stereotypical thinking. To supplement conversations within families, organizations like the Straight Spouse Network, PFLAG, and COLAGE are valuable resources. For those who are put off by the idea of meeting people face-to-face, the Internet is an invaluable tool for helping families find information while maintaining their privacy.

Transforming Laws, Cultivating Acceptance

For LGBT families to have rights equal to straight families, laws will have to evolve to include them. Is it most effective to influence law-making by transforming attitudes first? Or should laws be changed first in the hope that community standards will follow?

The arguments from homo-hostile people who oppose laws that protect LGBT families are usually made on moral rather than practical grounds. In a debate on the radio, I heard a homo-hostile legislator making his case against second-parent adoption for same-sex parents. He was fully aware of how prohibiting this legal procedure penalizes the children of gay parents. He did not directly condone denying these children their rights, but instead focused on what would be communicated *morally* if government chose to protect LGBT families. Whatever anti-gay politicians may think about sexuality, making sure that LGBT families are no less vulnerable than straight families does not mean that they are making a statement condoning anything. Making same-sex marriage legal does not require an anti-gay politician to attend gay weddings. Legalizing second-parent adoption doesn't mean a lesbian couple is going to ask their homophobic senator to be the baby's godparent.

On the other hand, homo-hostile people know that when laws are changed, it has an impact on overall social thinking. In its decision on *Lawrence v. Texas*, for example, the Supreme Court declared that anti-sodomy laws were unconstitutional, freeing gay people from the label of "criminal" in all fifty states. The ruling in June 2003 immediately sparked widespread public discourse about same-sex marriage and family rights.

Laws that extend equal rights to queer families make a statement about the validity of such families whether or not that is the intent of lawmakers. If these families are granted access that is equal to straight families in hospital rooms, workplaces, courtrooms, and funeral homes, a stronger case can be made for their inclusion in churches, neighbor-hoods, and car pools. More homo-hesitant people will realize that "those people" are not really "those people" after all, but rather their friends, neighbors, clients, coworkers, and classmates. It will be in-creasingly difficult to make a case as to why "those people" are so im-moral. The acceptance of LGBT families is a gradual process that will be realized with vigilance and persistence. It will be the result of indi-vidual families making themselves visible to change the stereotypes in homo-hesitant minds, one person at a time.

Heterosexual people who are willing to learn about the need for equality can become valuable and effective allies in the struggle to amend laws and transform minds. They need to be included in the dis-cussion, and LGBT families need to show them *how* they can help. It starts with our family members.

For homo-hesitant family members, silence might be the "easiest" option during awkward moments. Silence, however, comes at a cost for the entire family. Even when LGBT family members learn to ig-nore oversights, their children rarely do. They internalize the message that their part of the family is less valid. They begin to question the sincerity of their relationships with cousins, uncles, aunts, and grand-parents.

Talking openly about everyday homophobia informs family and friends about how LGBT families need their support to challenge both legal and social discrimination. The conversations about equality that we start in our living rooms pave the way for the continuation of these conversations in Congress.

Six

Silent Panic:
The Impact of HIV/AIDS on
Children of Gay Parents

*If only I had known anyone with a gay HIV-positive parent when
my father was sick, dying, and after, it would have made a huge
difference. . . . The epidemic is different now than ten years ago,
but the children are still afraid and isolated.*
—JENNY LADEN, 32

"I talked to Jim today," I remember hearing my father tell Russ back
when I was in junior high. "He says Steven is not well."

Not well. I knew what that meant. I was not sure who Steven was,
but I knew my dad was saying that Steven had AIDS. Dad and Russ
rarely said the actual name of the disease. I followed their cue and
avoided saying the word. Although Dad and Russ did not have AIDS,
the disease was a backdrop in my family. They talked "over" me to
minimize the impact of the epidemic on my life, but their avoidance
only increased my fears and my feelings of helplessness.

The wave of gay men dying from AIDS in the 1980s and 1990s
has subsided, but AIDS is still a presence in gay communities. New
treatments have slowed down death rates, resulting in the population
of people living with AIDS increasing each year. In 1994, an esti-
mated 95,000 men who have sex with men were living with
HIV/AIDS; five years later, the estimate had increased to 143,000.[17]

This is not to imply that AIDS is a "gay disease." It is not my intention to revive old myths that only gay men will get AIDS, but reported cases of gay and bisexual men with HIV are on the rise again following a steady decline in the late 1990s. According to the Centers for Disease Control and Prevention (CDC), diagnosed cases of HIV among men who have sex with men increased 7.1 percent in 2002. It was the third year in a row that diagnosed cases in this population rose, with a cumulative increase of nearly 18 percent since 1999.[18]

The CDC suggests that this upward trend is due in part to younger generations of gay and bisexual men who have no memories of what it was like in gay communities when so many people were getting sick and dying.[19] Now, because of early detection and new treatments, people living with AIDS stay healthier longer, and the telltale physical signs of AIDS are rare. Without firsthand experiences of the epidemic, it's easier to be in denial or to grow complacent. But when it comes to AIDS, denial and complacency can be life-threatening.

Grown children of gay parents know the reality of AIDS. Like other survivors of the epidemic, they do not want this history repeated. But amid the stories of men taking care of dying lovers and parents mourning the loss of their sons, people who have lost gay parents to AIDS are rarely acknowledged. The major reason for their invisibility is because of concerns about how AIDS could influence limitations on gay parenting. For opponents to gay parenting, AIDS is the reason that gay men should not be allowed to parent, on the grounds that children of gay parents are more likely to be orphaned or infected. This homophobic linking of AIDS to parental rights prevents children from being open about a parent's HIV status—even within LGBT communities.

Such self-censoring prevents sons and daughters from seeking support, and it prevents social services from understanding that this group needs support. With HIV-positive people living years longer, AIDS has become a more manageable disease for those who have access to good health care. Still, families that are affected struggle with the stigma of the disease, feelings of isolation, the demanding medical regimen, the financial strain, and the complexities of telling people— who, when, and how. The number of children with gay parents who are HIV-positive is unknown, but Alysia Abbott, 32, whose father died in 1992, says, "We are a small group but . . . a real demographic, and as much deserving of compassion and community as the more visible and typical demographics."

Whether or not they have parents with AIDS, the threat of the disease compromises children's security, causing them to wonder if or when their parents will get sick. Children growing up with gay fathers, uncles, and godparents know AIDS as an ever-present fear. Their awareness of the disease starts earlier than it does for their peers from straight families. "Though many queerspawn will never know firsthand the experience of a parent living or dying with AIDS, queerspawn do feel vulnerable in a way that children of straight parents don't," says Alysia. "The statistics and the popular conceptions tell you that your gay father may contract and die of AIDS. Long before my father actually tested HIV-positive, I lived with the fear that he would."

Just because children are not asking parents about HIV doesn't mean they are not thinking about it. Parents need to address the issue of HIV and assure children that they are protecting themselves. This does not necessarily have to be a conversation devoted solely to HIV; the subject can be brought up in a discussion of safer sex in general.[20] Parents need to take the lead in starting these conversations; it is often too difficult for their children to initiate them. "I don't think that I could have the 'safe sex' conversation with my father," says Sarah Larkin, 20, "but I think it would help me to feel reassured. His choices don't just affect himself; they affect me and my family. Three people have died in my family from AIDS. And I hope it stops there."

THE LONG SHADOW OF AIDS

It's always difficult when a parent dies. Parents die from many causes: car crashes, heart attacks, cancer. But a gay parent's death from AIDS is different. Stefan Lynch, 31, who was fifteen when his stepfather died and nineteen when his father died, says children with HIV-positive gay parents share a specific experience:

> These are often not typical "kids losing a parent" stories be-
> cause they are occurring in the context of a community-wide
> epidemic. That means that a kid often has seen other people
> die of the same disease . . . and that this is a fear that they may
> have lived with and planned for emotionally for years, often
> long before a diagnosis. I grew up thinking I would be dead by
> thirty and planning my life that way. That's just how things
> were for young men in my community.

Jenny Laden, 32, paid close attention to AIDS years before she learned her dad was positive. She did research projects on the epidemic both in high school and college. "I knew a lot about the disease probably because my father was gay," Jenny says, "but I didn't think he was going to get it. It was just something that I was interested in. I was paying attention to it in the media. I don't remember consciously worrying about my father getting AIDS, but maybe on some level I did."

Even if their parents were not diagnosed, children still saw them involved in activism around the issue: fundraising, support groups, phone trees, hospice caregiving, and condom distribution. Jon's gay dad did not contract HIV, but Jon was very aware of the virus because his father ran the local gay crisis line from their home. "Other kids were not keyed into it the way we were," says Jon, 30. "By the time I was in junior high, I knew people who had AIDS. That was good for me, because I wasn't afraid of it. It wasn't just this thing I had seen on TV. It was real."

Gay-parent families today have an advantage over families in the 1980s in that they have a lot more information about AIDS and its transmission. When adult children first learned about AIDS, it was something they overheard in a conversation or in a news report about a "gay cancer." All we knew was that the disease was killing gay men. Families worried that children would contract AIDS from their fathers. Nancy, 30, talks about how this fear affected her family:

> Sometime around 1985, my brother and I were about to leave for a trip to visit my father in San Francisco. My mother was apprehensive about letting us go. This was a time when everyone thought that just being around a gay man would give you AIDS. People were worried about sitting on toilet seats in public restrooms and using silverware in restaurants that gay people may have used. My mom let us go, but my dad had to promise to wash the dishes really well and not kiss us on the lips.

Debates raged about whether the disease was punishment for the sin of homosexuality, with homo-hostile people touting AIDS as the express trip to hell that gay men deserved. This mentality was condoned with silence from the White House as the death toll rose. (Hence the ACT UP slogan "Silence = Death.") President Reagan did not address AIDS or even publicly say the name of the disease until 1987.

I interpreted the silence in the most personal way: *Gay people don't count and we don't care if your dad dies.*

At the same time, in my high school, AIDS was only a joke. Literally.

What do you call Rock Hudson on a skateboard? Roll-AIDS.

Classmates who had long grown out of the phase of worrying about boy-germs and girl-germs reverted to teasing one another about AIDS like it was a new form of cooties.

Get away from me before you give me AIDS!

My peers' ignorance enraged me. I *knew* I could shut them up if I told them how AIDS was not as removed from them as they thought. But by doing that, I was afraid they would figure out my dad was gay. And then what? They would assume that because my dad was gay, he also had AIDS. Would people stop talking to me? Be afraid to be in the same room with me? The idea of people thinking my father was infected conjured up images akin to the final scenes in the movie *E.T.*— dozens of silent quick-moving men in silver spacesuits appearing out of nowhere to seal up our house with my dad inside.

I braced myself for the news that my father has never delivered. I thought it was a matter of when—not if—he contracted the virus.

In my midtwenties, my then boyfriend said he thought it was "morbid" that I turned first to the obituaries whenever I opened the newspaper. I hadn't really noticed until he said something about it. It was an old habit: combing the listings, looking for young unmarried men with no cause of death mentioned, and only an occasional reference to an AIDS organization designated for memorial donations. Finding the clues was my private way of honoring the dead; making sure they had not died unnoticed.

In 1999, a friend asked me to volunteer with her for a bike ride that raised funds for AIDS research. At first I was repelled by the idea. I was tired of AIDS; it didn't seem like an issue that affected me since I didn't know anyone who was HIV-positive. But after I thought about it, I was flooded with memories about how AIDS had affected my childhood. My strongest memories were from Dad and Russ's involvement with the Twin Cities Gay Men's Chorus. The chorus lost dozens of members to AIDS, and my awareness of this grew into an expectation that someone else was going to be getting sick. Watching the men around me take care of dying friends, bury them, and then rally their forces for the next person's dignified death had a long-lasting effect on me. I had never shared my feelings about AIDS with my parents because I thought they did not want to talk about it. Anyway, I figured that watching their friends die was already enough for them to deal with.

I had thought that because my parents did not contract the virus, I did not have a right to consider myself "affected" by the epidemic. After talking with other children with gay dads, both HIV-positive and negative, I saw that I was only denying how I had been affected and suppressing my feelings. When I really let myself think about it, I realized the reason I didn't know of anyone who was HIV-positive was that those who were positive had died years earlier. I also found that there were indeed positive people around me, but I didn't know their status because they were successfully maintaining their health.

Dad and Russ and I sometimes joke that even though I am heterosexual, I am "gayer" than they are. They have few gay friends and rarely attend LGBT community functions. I am the one who stays apprised of LGBT events and issues and I often have to fill them in on the latest. Underneath our joking is the tacit understanding that they would be more involved in the gay community if more people from their old social networks were still alive.

The impact of AIDS has also contributed to seemingly unrelated long-term changes on LGBT communities. One example is the solidarity that now exists between gay men and lesbian women for political and community organizing. In the early 1980s, when the government was dismissing AIDS as a "gay disease," gay men drew from the organizing skills of the women's health cooperatives to help them meet the

152 Families Like Mine

community needs that the government ignored. Nowadays, young queer activists on university campuses take it for granted that men and women work together. They find it hard to believe how separate lesbian and gay communities were just a couple decades ago. Men and women working together to fight AIDS also had a direct impact on creating queer families in new ways. "Without the breaking down of the huge gap between lesbians and gay men that AIDS entailed," Stefan points out, "we would not be seeing so many blended queer families." That is, gay men and lesbian women creating biological children that they co-parent in nonromantic partnerships.

TALKING TO SONS AND DAUGHTERS ABOUT HIV STATUS

When a parent discovers he is HIV-positive, he faces the challenge of disclosing his status not only to friends and past and current lovers, but also to his children. The process of talking about HIV status is similar to the process of coming out, in terms of the anxiety and doubts it engenders: *Will they blame me? Will they disown me? Will they still love me?* Regardless of their initial reaction, most children prefer to know rather than not know. Whenever possible, it will be less scary for children—of any age—to learn about a parent's status before the parent is visibly sick. This gives them time to adjust to the news rather than learning at the time of a medical crisis.

Kirk Wisland, 30, was fifteen when his father told him he was positive. Back then, Kirk and his family saw the diagnosis as a death sentence. "The questions going around in my head weren't about how he was going to stay healthy. They were more like, 'Is he going to make it to my high school graduation?'" Kirk did not voice any of the questions he wanted to ask because his father's partner at the time was present. "I wasn't that close to his partner, so I felt incredibly uncomfortable. I would have felt more comfortable asking questions if my dad had told me when we were alone." Kirk's father has been living with HIV since 1984.

When Jenny's father told her, "He basically said, 'I hate to tell you this but I'm HIV-positive.' . . . I was really scared, very, very sad, and just freaked out. . . . I had to face this unknown: that he could be around for two years or for twenty."

Like a gay parent who remains closeted, an HIV-positive parent who does not disclose his status to his children puts enormous energy into hiding his secret, thereby bringing tension into the parent-children relationship. Jenny says that her father decided to tell her and her brother after a friend who had not told him he had AIDS died. "His friend hadn't let my dad be a part of that process," Jenny says, "something that they could go through together. [My dad] suddenly realized that that's what he was doing to me and my brother."

If parents are noticeably sick, keeping the secret from their children means they have to distance themselves physically. After Nancy had not seen her father for three years, he came to town to attend her high school graduation and to tell her he had full-blown AIDS. "I remember not really being surprised," says Nancy, "because it was something we had feared for a long time. But it was more a feeling of sadness that my father didn't feel that he could tell us sooner and that he had wasted a lot of time not talking to us at all. . . . I was never ashamed of my dad for being gay or getting AIDS and I really felt a need to make sure he knew that."

Other parents hide their HIV-status from their children because they don't want to come out as gay. Gina, 26, was seventeen when she learned her dad was gay on the same day he told her he had AIDS. She had grown up with her mother in another state and rarely saw her father. Gina was considering attending the University of Minnesota, in part because her father lived in Minneapolis and she saw this as an opportunity to build a relationship with him. While visiting the campus the summer before her senior year in high school, she went to see her father, who was obviously very sick. When he told her he had AIDS, she was nearly speechless, but still found the courage to ask, "Are you gay?" She recalls her reaction:

> I did not feel it was appropriate to ask a lot of questions [about his sexuality] as I was more in shock about his AIDS status. He was my father and nothing else mattered. I asked, "Why didn't you tell me sooner?" I will never forget the words that came out of his mouth. . . . He said, "I thought that you wouldn't love me anymore." This is the number one thing that most people in life worry about; that someone will not love them. It's a shame that even a father could not be open and honest without fear of rejection.

Gina's father died three months later.

Daniel Lessem, 28, was fourteen when his father got sick. Even when his father was hospitalized, his family kept the reason vague, saying it had to do with "bacteria in the blood." Since his father was a dentist, his family feared that his patients would react to the news hysterically, and perhaps even initiate lawsuits. Knowing that he was not being told the truth about what was wrong with his own father was confusing and frustrating for Daniel:

> I understand the depth of their precautions more now as an adult, but back then I felt as if my brother and I were left in [the] lurch. My father made little to no effort to discuss his illness with me, and I felt he lacked courage or interest to do so. Fortunately, he opened up to me as he began to deteriorate. Eventually we did have a few opportunities to talk about his

dying, his lifestyle as a closeted bisexual man, his first experiences, his resentment for the loss of his life, and his participation within the family which would outlive him.

Some parents and their children don't ever talk about it. Danny Crosby was twenty-one when his father died in 1993. His siblings had cut off all contact with their dad and changed their names after they learned he was gay. Danny was the only one who was with his dad in the final year of his life. Danny's father never mentioned he had AIDS, but told his son he had cancer.

"I never questioned him about it," Danny says, "I just remember visiting him in the hospital and it was obvious that it was an AIDS ward." He thinks that parents should tell their children as soon as they are old enough to understand, "otherwise they will figure it out on their own."

HIV-positive parents who have already disclosed their status to their children are sometimes inclined to try to hide the progression of the virus. In the long run, however, *not* having this information can cause additional anxiety. Jenny appreciated that her father kept her well informed throughout his illness:

> I felt like my father was telling me [details about his health] as a way for that experience to be both of ours. His message was, "We're going to get through this together." That made me feel loved and cared about. As awful and as frightening as it was, at least it meant we were a team. We had each other. That helped a lot.

Since Kirk's dad has lived with the virus so long, he and Kirk rarely talk about it. But during periods over the last twenty years when his health had been more fragile, he gave Kirk regular updates. "There have been times when he's told me 'my T-cells are this' or 'the doctor said that.' He has kept me well apprised of all that was going on." Kirk appreciated his father's honesty; it kept him from assuming the worst. "Parents need to find a balance between not alarming their kids and not hiding the truth," adds Kirk. "I would have been annoyed if he had said everything was fine when it wasn't."

How much information a parent should share depends on the child. One child might want regular updates, while another one might not want to hear about it unless there is an emergency. The level of information will probably vary with the developmental stage of the child. Some children who are living in another state or away at college avoid thinking about it, while others feel an even stronger need to know the details while they are gone. Stefan reminds HIV-positive parents: "Don't assume that because you are inundated with information about AIDS, protease inhibitors, prophylactic treatments, and lipodystrophy, that your kids know diddly."

If you are HIV-positive and unsure how much information your children want, *ask them*.

SUPPORTING CHILDREN WITH HIV-POSITIVE PARENTS

Children with HIV-positive parents need support for the issues that are unique to them. They have their own worries and stresses related to the status of their parents, and it helps when parents validate the children's feelings. "[My father] was very understanding of my process," says Jenny, "really respecting and honoring that I was going through some things as well, that it wasn't just him."

Among the issues is that of having to live with the unknowns of a disease—not knowing how to plan for the future. Children with HIV-positive parents also struggle with disclosure about their parents' status. They need to know if it is safe to tell friends, and they also need help finding ways to talk about the subject with their friends. As with coming out, peer reactions are a source of anxiety. When Gina told her boyfriend that her father had AIDS, she says that "he was so in shock and scared that he dumped me and would not even see me. It was quite difficult at the time, because I was scared that I would lose more people [who] loved me like I lost my boyfriend."

Depending on a child's knowledge of how a parent contracted the virus, the child could be dealing with anger toward the parent in addition to sadness. Perhaps the child was told (or assumed) a parent was being monogamous when he really was not. Or maybe the anger is toward a father's partner, who was having unprotected sex outside of the partnership.

These feelings are even more overwhelming if children with married parents learn that a parent has contracted the disease from a spouse who has been closeted. Daniel remembers finding out that his mother was HIV-positive, and knowing that it was his father who had passed on the virus to her. "I wasn't fully aware of exactly how he kept his homosexual activities from my mom," Daniel remembers, "yet the idea of there being hidden agendas in his social life was appalling and disgusting. . . . I was a part of his social agenda as his son, and my mother as his wife. I felt we deserved better than being misled by him just so he could get off. And as a result, my mother was HIV-positive; that disturbed me to no end."

Children should not have to sort through this kind of information on their own. Private counselors not only need to be HIV-savvy, they also must meet the needs and style of the child. Children must be reassured that the person they are going to talk to is not homophobic. Melanie Gates, 29, had a terrible experience when she thought she was going to someone she could count on for support while her father was dying. "My mom took me to the pastor at our church," explains Melanie. "He informed me that God used AIDS as a punishment for gay people and that I should be okay with it because it was God's will. Needless to say, I am not religious now."

Parents need to explore resources on behalf of their children, and let them know that it is not a sign of weakness or family betrayal to seek support outside of their family. Age-appropriate books and pamphlets about HIV can also be helpful—*anything* that reflects their experience can help decrease the isolation.

As parents become so sick that they cannot care for themselves, teens and young adults often play active roles in the caretaking. When Alysia's father told her he was sick, they agreed that she would graduate early from college in New York City and return to San Francisco to care for him. After graduation Alysia felt torn between moving in order to be with her father and staying in New York, where she was settling into a new life she had created for herself—and was just beginning to enjoy. Her father wrote to tell her: "New York will still be there in a year. I might not be."

"AIDS was an abstract concept when I was living my life in New York," Alysia recalls, "but my dad was living with it every day. Not until I moved in with him and we met with doctors who were talking about his final stages of life did it hit me that he really was going to die."

Being a caretaker for a dying loved one is both physically and emotionally draining. Alysia joined a support group of caregivers in which she was only one of two women, and easily the youngest. The group was welcoming to her, but her unique experience of caring for a parent set her apart:

A lot of the nonparents in LGBT communities have friends or lovers who have suffered from AIDS. Having a parent with AIDS is more complicated. This is the person who was supposed to care for me and now I'm caring for him. I didn't choose this situation. I was born into it. I can't break up with this person. I can't drift and let our friendship fade out. This is my parent and mixed up with the illness and the dying is the complicated parent-child drama.

Resources at AIDS organizations are already stretched thin, but these service providers must understand how support for sons and daughters should be specific to their needs. "Typical AIDS support groups are not set up to deal with kids at all," says Stefan. "They can be alienating instead of helpful."

WHEN A PARENT DIES

At a time in their lives when sons and daughters are in control of very little, they should be able to decide how involved they want to be in a parent's dying. Some children are grateful to be with their parent during the final stages. Others feel fortunate not to have death be the final memory of their parent. "Because of my age," Gina says, "I was not ready to help someone die. I remember praying to God, and asking Him to not let my father die in front of me."

Children need to understand ahead of time that people in the final stage of life might not be coherent, may not recognize their own children, and might say things that they don't mean. One son wrote me years after his father's death, distressed that the last thing his father told him was that he had been a bad son. Even though he wants to believe his father didn't mean what he said, the father seemed so lucid that his words have haunted his son for years.

When one person in a gay couple dies, the surviving partner can choose whether or not to remain involved in the gay community. His network, much of it tested and strengthened during the final stages of his partner's life, is there for him as he grieves. If this network does not make a point of reaching out to the surviving children, their loss feels lonelier. Gina describes her experience:

I felt like an outsider at my own father's funeral. My father's partner received all of the hugs, all of the comfort from friends and family, and all of the sympathy cards. Out of all the friends or people [who] came to the funeral, I think that I knew four people. These were people . . . I had met before, and *none* of them attempted to approach me and give their condolences. I just sat watching as everyone approached my dad's partner.

It's probable that they didn't deliberately exclude her, but that they did not know what to do or say. Gina just needed what her father's partner needed: hugs and support.

The death of a father can also result in the loss of a relationship with another important person in the children's life: the father's partner. If the relationship is not clearly defined, the surviving partner and surviving children may drift apart as a result of deep grief or misunderstandings. Some surviving partners assume that children are not interested in maintaining a relationship with them after the parent has died. Others think that keeping the children in their lives would be a hindrance to moving on. This can be very painful for children who feel close to their father's partner or want to be around the person who was closest to their dad. I met a brother and sister who so badly wanted to keep their father's partner in their lives that they had not given up hope after twelve years. They were teens when their dad died, and his partner failed to maintain communication with them. They still send him cards and photographs to assure him he can contact them if he changes his mind.

Even after a parent dies, the fact that he died of AIDS means that people often react differently than they would if he had died from another cause. Jenny says, "On top of all this mourning and grief, you have this weird stigma you have to deal with."

Some of that stigma—and even hostility—comes from extended-family members who are either ashamed their relative was gay, that he contracted the virus, or both. "When the news was spread to my extended family about my dad's death," Nancy recalls, "I was dumbfounded by the reaction of one of my uncles. He said something like, 'It's about time that faggot dropped dead. He deserved to die of AIDS.'"

Amber Love, 25, has parents who are lesbian, but she still felt the impact of shame in her family when she was ten and her uncle died of AIDS in their small town in 1988. "Only a few nurses would care for him and only one doctor would treat him. My grandparents had us tell everyone he only had liver cancer, which I knew—even when I first found out in second grade—was a dumb, ignorant lie. I was outraged for him and I still am."

Talking openly about losing a loved one to AIDS can be difficult even years later. Melanie remains cautious about whom she tells about her father, because people do not know how to react. "I would say that there were and still are instances when I am not welcome to talk about these issues because my family or friends feel uncomfortable with the information."

Sometimes even people who would like to be supportive don't know what to say. "I feel like my story gets so sensationally dramatic that people don't know how to react," Alysia says. "Their awkwardness becomes burdensome to me. Lots of times, I just don't want to deal with it."

Jenny thinks the best way for children to handle their grief is to find others who have been through the same experience. Her first conversation with someone who had also lost a parent to AIDS was at a party. Jenny remembers the woman telling her, "I know this isn't the time to talk about it, but my dad also died of AIDS. If you ever want to talk about it, I'd be happy to." They jumped into a conversation that did not end until four in the morning. "Having someone with that common experience was amazingly helpful," Jenny says.

Melanie would like to speak with other people whose parents have died from AIDS. "I know for sure that I am not the only person in this world who experienced what I did. But I have never met anyone who has been able to say, 'I know exactly what that was like,' and really mean it."

IMPACT ON SEXUALITY

Children who came of age in communities that were disproportionately affected by AIDS were profoundly changed by the experience in terms of the way they view their own sexuality and desires. Not surprisingly, they often equate sex with deadly consequences. "AIDS added a dimension that made sex dangerous," says Diana, 30, whose father died in 1992. "Sex is love and sex can kill you—the ultimate dichotomy. For my father, AIDS was about shame. He saw it as punishment for being gay. It created additional shame inside me about my sexuality and my own desire."

Children in today's LGBT families have never known a time before AIDS. Many adult sons and daughters, however, grew up while the epidemic was unfolding. They were becoming or thinking about becoming sexually active around the time that many of their parents or parents' friends were being diagnosed. When I was fifteen, my friend got a prescription for birth control pills in anticipation of having sex with her boyfriend. It dawned on me that I was so preoccupied with AIDS I had nearly forgotten pregnancy was also a potential consequence of sex.

Daniel was sixteen, and beginning to question his own sexuality, when his father was dying:

It was a delicate and sexually confusing stage . . . new sexual desires for other boys [were] flooding my mind just as hormones began raging through my body. All the while my dad was dying a slow and shameful death. I felt betrayed by my father for leaving me just as I began to recognize how much we were alike. I felt betrayed by life itself for giving me such desires at a time when these same desires would ultimately take my father away from me.

Some sons and daughters admit they went through a period of sexual promiscuity when a parent was very ill or shortly after he died. They were left feeling self-destructive and fatalistic, asking themselves, "What do I care? We're all going to die anyway." Other caring adults should be aware of how this stage of grief may lead to unprotected sex. During this vulnerable time, sons and daughters can benefit from being gently reminded that they still owe it to themselves to avoid high-risk behavior.

Longer term, however, many of them become fierce opponents of sex without condoms outside of a committed relationship. They develop high expectations for honesty and communication with sexual partners, and are prepared to walk away from sexual encounters if their requests for protection are not respected. In those rare moments when unprotected sex "just happens," they feel extreme guilt and shame. Jenny, who now teaches HIV prevention workshops, speaks frankly about the occasions when she had unprotected sex:

> When I didn't use a condom . . . I was mortified afterward. I could count those times on one hand, but it definitely happened to me and I feel terrible about it. It weighs on me heavily—probably more so than someone who hasn't had a father die from AIDS. It's led me to a place of being more protective of myself sexually. There have been a few times when a man who I was sleeping with would try to keep going, and I'd be like, "What are you doing? Get a condom." It was always a

weird moment, especially if it was someone who didn't know my history. And then I drop the bomb about why I care so much about using condoms. That would ruin the mood immediately.

Like Jenny, other sexually active adult children commonly report having a sexual partner try to talk them out of using condoms. They talk about ending relationships or stopping sexual encounters because of disagreements about safer sex. Diana recalls, "I was with this guy, and I told him to put on a condom. He said, 'I'd prefer not to use one.' He *preferred* to not use one? I wanted to say, 'Fuck you, my dad died of AIDS.'"

The decision to practice safer sex is not just about protecting themselves. It's also about community responsibility. Robyn's gay father did not contract AIDS, but two of her uncles did. "After my dad's brothers died of AIDS," Robyn, 27, says, "I remember being afraid for my dad, hoping he was HIV-negative, and that he was practicing safe sex. It may sound strange, but I knew I couldn't control my dad and his sex life, so I made a promise to myself to be very safe in my own sex life when I grew up."

Because these children have seen the impact of one person's HIV status on an entire family, they know that the choices they make for themselves affect the people who care about them. Each time a son or daughter avoids high-risk sexual behavior they are making a conscious choice to take care of themselves so that they can stay alive and healthy for their loved ones.

CONTINUING TO ADVOCATE AND EDUCATE

Sons and daughters often get involved in AIDS-related activities— bike-ride fundraisers, meal delivery to people with AIDS, AIDS education workshops—as a way to do something in a situation over which they have no control. Children's awareness and dedication to stopping AIDS also occurs on more personal levels. Jenny says that in addition to leading workshops, she shares the information she gained from her family's experience less formally. She continues to be concerned about people whose sense of invincibility makes them vulnerable to transmission.

"There's a lot of ignorance around HIV and AIDS, especially among straight people," Jenny says. "One of my girlfriends contracted HIV at twenty-nine, so I sent out an e-mail to all my friends, saying, 'Look, I didn't get this information in school. You probably didn't either. And I want to make sure you have the facts.'"

Melanie, who is now a teacher, recently spoke up to enlighten some of her coworkers in the teachers' lounge who were saying they did not think school was an appropriate place for discussing gay issues. Melanie told them her father was gay, and after her colleagues apologized, she added that he had died of AIDS.

"This sent a chill through the air," Melanie remembers. "Every single one of them seemed to be uncomfortable with it. One of them finally said that she had never met anyone who even knew someone who had died of AIDS, let alone a close family member. They were all curious about how that felt and how I found out."

By explaining to her fellow teachers how she felt, she showed them how disallowing gay issues to be discussed in schools hurts students. "The one comment that stood out was what one of them said as she left: 'Wow, that must have been really hard and really isolating.'" No longer can Melanie's coworkers assume these issues do not affect the people around them.

After her father's death, Alysia faced the difficult transition of returning to her life in New York. Her experience of taking care of her father as he died was one of the first topics she would bring up when she met someone new. "I couldn't really get around it," she says. "I remember wishing that I could have included taking care of my dad on my résumé when I was job hunting because it was the most significant experience I had had in my life." Ten years after her father's death, she says, "I have so many other ways to define myself now."

Alysia observes the anniversary of her father's death with public readings of his writings and letters they sent to each other. She also started a website in her father's memory, www.steveabbott.org, to "remember my father in a very public way." While she created the site in order to put a face on AIDS, so that her father would not fade into the statistics, the on-line memorial also serves as a document of how a family—not just an individual—was affected by AIDS.

A few years back I hosted a gathering of teen and adult kids of gay and lesbian parents in my home. I knew that at least two of the ten people there had HIV-positive fathers, and another one's dad had died. Yet when we went around the circle introducing ourselves, none of them mentioned HIV. Afterward, I spoke to each one privately, and found out that all three had deliberately censored themselves. Each said they didn't want to be "the one" to reinforce the stereotype that a dad who is gay is likely to have AIDS. They didn't want to be "the one" at the meeting to deflate the group's enthusiasm. All three were surprised to find out that they weren't the only one, as they were so used to assuming. If one had spoken up, the two others (and perhaps more I wasn't aware of) would have known there was someone they could talk to who shared this experience. Children of gay parents need reassurance that the impact of AIDS on families does not have to be a secret.

The threat of AIDS continues. Ignoring its impact on families will not make it go away, but talking about it can alleviate some of the anxiety and isolation. Many children—even those with parents who are HIV-negative—internalize the grief, fear, and shame that still surround the epidemic. When those feelings are suppressed, they impede communication in families. Some parents resist the idea of talking about

AIDS, safer sex or their HIV status, because they believe that their sexual decisions should not be their children's concern. Granted, it is not necessary for parents to share the details of their sex life, but the private, sexual choices parents make affect their children nonetheless.

Gay parents raising children today must understand the critical connection between safer sex and parenthood. Unprotected sex is not just physically risky; it also puts children at risk of losing a parent. Children of HIV-negative parents want to know that their parents are protecting themselves to minimize their risk. Children with HIV-positive parents need to decide for themselves how much their parents should inform them about the disease's progression. In either case, children deserve to know the truth about the HIV status of their parents.

Seven

Second Generation:
Queer Kids of LGBT Parents

When queer parents want to highlight well-adjusted children to prove how normal our families are, "well adjusted" is often a euphemism for "straight."
                    —DAN CHERUBIN, 38

A few years ago, I listened to the hosts of a morning radio show as they ridiculed *Daddy's Roommate*, an affirming picture book about a young boy whose dad is gay. Neither the callers nor the hosts had even seen the book, but they mocked the very concept of gay parents. I called in, naively thinking they would listen to me and show a little compassion. I told them what the book meant to me and attempted to address their specific criticisms.

Predictably, the novelty of a real live person with a gay dad immediately shifted the focus of the conversation to the topic of my sexual orientation. Despite my attempts to evade their questions about my sexuality, they persisted until I could not see a way around answering them. As soon as I told them I was heterosexual, their accusing tone softened; the verbal equivalent of putting their swords back into their sheaths. With their opportunity for sensationalism derailed, I was promptly disconnected. I regretted not thinking fast enough to reply, "And so what if I *were* gay?" I felt nauseated, disappointed in myself for not handling "the question" better.

It's the question pondered and at times obsessed over by gay advocates and opponents, researchers, media, and LGBT parents themselves: Do gay parents make their children gay? When I am presenting to a room full of new LGBT parents and I address this question, many are relieved to hear that contrary to what anti-gay rhetoric would like everyone to believe, their children will not automatically grow up to be gay.[21] Some parents make special note of this factoid so they can use it to quell their own parents' worries or defend their families during homophobic debates. The dialogue around this issue, however, needs to go beyond simply reassuring everyone that children of gay parents are no more or less likely to be gay than any other children. The discussion needs to be extended to ask why it matters at all. The preoccupation with this issue has more to do with homophobia, stereotypes, and politics than with innocent curiosity.

As I explained in Chapter One, the impetus for conducting research on children of gay and lesbian parents was to defend the custody and visitation rights of gay parents leaving heterosexual marriages. Judges tended to favor the straight parent over the gay parent, based on prejudiced assumptions about gay people, including the assumption that they will raise their children to be gay. In response, lawyers introduced studies to challenge that assumption. Unfortunately, the pressure to cite such research for the sake of helping gay parents keep their children continually reinforces the societal assumption that it's better to be heterosexual. Implicit in such arguments is the suggestion that the rights of future gay parents depend on current gay parents' ability to produce heterosexual children. Emphasizing the research findings to make a case for gay parenting rights sends an unspoken homophobic message: "Don't penalize the gay parents—they don't bring any more queers into the world than straight parents do."

While talking on the phone with my dad, I shared with him the excitement I felt after a meeting with a group of adult children of queer parents. Dad asked how many of the eleven people at the meeting were heterosexual. Three, I told him. He inhaled a quick, audible breath and then whispered intensely into the phone, as if spies might overhear: "What does that say about the statistics?!" My dad's reaction is a fairly common one. LGBT parents fear that evidence of queer kids will not fare well under the scrutiny of anti-gay policy makers, and although such children exist, they should be acknowledged only within LGBT communities—and even then, only in whispers.

Neglected in the whispers are the children who actually do come out as LGBT. These sons and daughters, already challenged by the usual stigma in broader society for being queer, face an added stigma *within* their own LGBT community from people who fear their visibility will reinforce the stereotype. The history of homophobia shows why this fear exists, but it unfairly manifests into stigma that becomes the children's burden. This stigma against queer kids of queer parents perpetuates a cycle of shame around queerness—a cycle of shame that LGBT communities need to be committed to eliminating on all levels.

When people find out someone has LGBT parents, it is common for them to think they are entitled to ask about the child's sexual orientation. These days I am asked more often because of my work, but the questions from peers began well before I entered junior high: "If your dad is gay, then what does that make you?" At first I didn't understand why they were asking. Why would my dad's attraction to men make me attracted to *women*? Where was the logic in that? I would give them an innocent answer, based on the crushes that preoccupied me in fourth and fifth grade: "I guess I like boys."

Then I started to pick up on what people were assuming. They were wondering if my father's gayness might have somehow influenced me or if gayness was genetic. Why should my sexual orientation be the basis for judging my father's worthiness as a parent? If I were gay, my father would be deemed guilty of forcing his so-called deviant lifestyle upon me, making it seep into my psyche and turn me queer. But if I remained unaffected by his corrupt ways and turned out heterosexual, he would be pardoned for reproducing. When I figured out why people were asking the question, I resented it and avoided answering whenever possible.

STRAIGHTENING UP FOR THE PUBLIC

While the homophobic assumption is that children of LGBT parents are pushed into "the homosexual lifestyle," in actuality, children often feel more pressure to identify as *straight*. This pressure means that at times LGBT children are not comfortable about being out, even at LGBT community events. For example, when I organize panels of daughters and sons to speak to parent groups, few queer kids of LGBT parents are willing to participate. Even among those who do agree to speak publicly, some omit their own sexual orientation from their family story because they do not want to make the audience of LGBT parents uncomfortable.

Jon, 30, who is straight, rarely talks openly with his parents or anyone else about having a gay dad and lesbian mom. Still, he grew up sensing that turning out heterosexual would reflect better on his parents. His father recently expressed interest in getting Jon involved in LGBT advocacy. Jon thinks his father's encouragement is in part due to his knowledge of the leverage straight children provide in the politics of LGBT family rights:

My dad said, "You're the perfect poster boy for gay parenting: straight, married, an attorney, good-looking. . . ." I think he was saying it a little tongue in cheek, but knowing my dad, I get the sense that he's glad that I'm straight. Mostly because he didn't want his kids to go through what he went through growing up. But what if I were gay? Would he be so into the idea of me being front and center on this stuff?

Because of the pressure to demonstrate that gay parents produce straight children, some LGBT families who initially agree to appear in media mysteriously fade out of the spotlight if, as their children mature, it appears that one of them might be queer. These children would be no less articulate or confident speaking to media than they'd been when they were younger, but their emerging sexuality makes families feel vulnerable to a negative judgment in a way they did not when the children were too young to be expected to address this question.

Sympathetic journalists think they are doing these families a favor by not drawing attention to them. One journalist told me she was planning to profile a particular teenager with gay parents but doubted her choice after he told her he was gay, too. A lesbian friend was trying to talk her out of it, saying, "Don't do that to us"—"us" meaning LGBT people who plan to become parents someday. It's as if one LGBT family with a gay child could be single-handedly responsible for destroying the progress of LGBT family rights.

Debra, 18, was raised with two mothers and also identifies as gay. She says that when she volunteers to talk to LGBT parent groups or to media, she feels like she is expected to prove that she is "okay":

> In my own mind, "okay" means a whole lot of things. But I think to other people, "okay" means straight. And although they don't come out and say that, I know [it], because in every interview I've been asked that question: "How do you define yourself?" I've always been asked that, by the media, by peers, by people I speak to in presentations.

Les Addison, 35, who was raised by her adoptive mother and partner, remembers how people reacted to her family when she came out about herself:

> I would find that my opinion about LGBT rights or equality was given more respect if I was seen as the daughter of a lesbian than if I was seen as a lesbian myself. I also found that in some situations, I had to choose who to be out about—Mom or me—because if someone realized that I was the lesbian daughter of a lesbian mom, they wanted to rush me onto *Jerry Springer*.

Jesse Gilbert, 30, who was raised by lesbian parents, is adamant about not declaring his sexual orientation at all. He says he will not dignify the public's homophobic quest to make conclusions about gay parents based on his answer:

> It's obvious that there's an assumption that there's a right and wrong answer to the question . . . if I'm invited to speak in the media, I'm not comfortable telling them about my own sexual orientation. I tell them so and why, but most often it gets edited out. In one piece [for television], they had someone from [a conservative, homo-hostile organization] who was saying these really inflammatory comments about parents making their kids gay. They wanted [the edited footage] to cut to my face and say, "No, I'm straight, no problem." The producer actually came to my house and gave me a lecture because she was so pissed. I wasn't answering their money question.

The media's insistence on getting an answer to the "money question" can be particularly upsetting for children who are questioning their sexuality or are in the process of coming out. Sarah Larkin, 20, was on a daytime talk show to discuss her experience growing up with a gay dad, but she was most worried about being asked about her own sexuality:

> That question, and only that question, was my downfall. I sat there, sweating and waiting for [the host of the show] to ask. It was the only thing I could focus on. I had inklings that I was a lesbian, but [I was] sort of in denial. If she had asked me, I would have lied and said I was straight. There are times when I would lie about it, or at least give a wishy-washy answer. I'd say something like, "I don't really think at this age that we should be pressured to define ourselves."

So dedicated are they to demonstrating that their parents and other gay people are "normal" that some queer kids of gay parents elect to stay in the closet about themselves when they speak to media. Debra is among the children who made that difficult choice. She was called by a reporter from a major daily newspaper and asked if she was interested in being profiled in an article about gay parenting. During the preliminary interview it became clear to Debra that the reporter wanted to feature a child who was heterosexual. Debra remembers:

> They were looking for someone [who] was as normal as normal could be. They wanted to say that all of this happened amazingly with gay parents and "isn't that amazing that it could happen like this?" But I don't think they would have done the article if I would have also said, "I might be the fun-loving all-American teenage kid you want me to be, and oh, by the way, I also have a girlfriend."

Debra agreed to the interview because she feels strongly about presenting positive images of gay parenting, and she didn't want her sexual orientation to ruin that opportunity. After the article ran, Debra felt conflicted about her decision:

> I felt really good about this really great lie. I was happy to know that maybe one more person would read the article and think gay people can be good parents. . . . I knew that portraying this really great image [of being heterosexual] was actually portraying this really big lie. Why do I do the things that I do? To open people's minds. But I didn't open anybody's mind, really. I wasn't the person that I felt they wanted me to be.

Several years have passed since that interview, but Debra is not yet comfortable being open about her own sexuality when she is speaking publicly about her family. She knows she is not the only one facing this dilemma. "I've read stories and stories about kids of gays," Debra explains. "Some of them I know personally and I know they are gay, too, but it's never said [that they are gay] in the articles. I think for kids of gays who want to change the world one article at a time, they feel the pressure to cover it up."

These gay kids feel torn, choosing between being honest about themselves or staying in the closet to present the preferred public image of their families. Children should not be put in the middle of this homophobic hypocrisy.

NAMING THE SECOND GENERATION

As a gay son of a lesbian mother, Dan Cherubin, has experienced first-hand a variety of reactions when people find out that both he and his mother are gay. He says that the reality of some children also being queer is mostly ignored, and typically when it is acknowledged "it's as if we are some interesting infectious disease." During one Pride parade

Dan marched in the family contingency with a sign that said GAY SON OF GAY MOMS. He watched LGBT parents' faces take on expressions that he was used to seeing on homophobic people—as if their children needed to be protected from him or that his gayness were contagious.

"Gay people, of all people, should know it's not something we choose," Dan says. To advocate for LGBT kids of LGBT parents, Dan founded Second Generation in 1992. The name of the group worked its way into queer-family lingo, providing a shorthand description for all LGBT kids of LGBT parents, not just those on Dan's member list.

At thirty-eight, Dan is now older than many LGBT parents. Despite the lukewarm receptions he often receives for his activism, he continues to be present and outspoken at LGBT family events—not just as a gay man, and not just as a son of a lesbian mom, but as a gay son of a lesbian mom. He says, "I feel the need to be there because it's a very amorphous concept [to LGBT parents] that their children will grow up to be adults." Adults who—Dan wants parents to understand—will not necessarily be heterosexual.

The coming-out process for second generation children is influenced by many family dynamics, including how closely they equate queerness with their parents. When children consider this association to be strong, some initially reject their own same-sex attractions in an attempt to define themselves independently of their family. This does not necessarily have to do with not wanting to be queer, but simply not wanting to be *like their parents*. Les explains:

> I think between the ages of thirteen and twenty-one I didn't want to be like them in any way at all. There were times when it was difficult to determine what was about my sexual orientation versus my mothers' sexual orientation. I think that some of my adolescent sexual experimentation with boys was a reaction to my mothers' sexuality, and a way to be "different from" [my mom and her partner]. Having lesbian moms made

me *more* interested in trying to be straight, rather than giving me permission to express my own sexuality.

Other children who experience a period of uncertainty find their anxiety compounded by the expectation that they should know definitively. It makes it all the more difficult for children to sort through which parts of their questioning are really about their own identities and which parts are about the politics. Greta, 24, whose mother is lesbian, says her constant awareness of how her sexuality mattered to people on a political level affected her process of figuring things out for herself:

I got asked this question so often by researchers and media people, so I have been questioning my sexuality my whole life. I never knew my sexuality until very late and was very asexual until recently. Last summer I thought I was straight because I had suddenly understood what people were talking about and started to look at guys the way you are "supposed" to. . . . I was also looking at girls much the same way. I have gradually and very slowly come out as bi.

Even after these children come out, people in LGBT communities do not necessarily "see" the sons and daughters as LGBT unless it is explicitly stated. Les explains how even though she did not hide her queer sexual orientation as an adult, her own identity was still overshadowed by her mother's:

When I was first coming out, there were people who knew that my mother was in a same-sex relationship, so they saw my expressions of support for LGBT rights as supporting her, my presence at gay bars as being about her, my interest in working for an organization supporting the legal rights of lesbian families as being about her . . . it made it harder for people to see me *as me*.

Laurie Cicotello, 32, whose father is transgender, also finds it challenging for her own identity to be recognized and validated independent of her father's identity. When Laurie mentions that she is bisexual in LGBT settings, she says reactions are "usually good, but it scares me. I am afraid that my message of being queerspawn will be lost if I tell people [I'm bisexual]."

When Laurie found the courage to come out to her father, she remembers her father's nonchalant reaction: "Yeah, so? Everyone is bisexual to some degree." Because of their differing views on the significance of Laurie's bisexuality, her father talks freely about it, while Laurie would prefer more discretion:

> [My parent] has often outed me to her friends, thinking that it was hilarious to have such a parenting situation. Of course, everyone was very accepting, but I felt violated inside. My issues are often pushed to the background because I'm afraid of "stealing" her spotlight. Perhaps someday I'll deal with my issues, but it's easier for me to ride on her coattails and be hush-hush about what I want in life and in relationships.

Laurie's concern that her coming-out will diminish or undermine her parent's identity is shared by other daughters and sons. Amber Love's mom and partner had lived together for years before they put words to their relationship. Their timing for officially coming out made Amber decide to postpone her own.

"I actually had worked up my nerve and was intending to come out my senior year of high school," says Amber, 25. "Then came my moms' official announcement, and really, a family celebration of being out as a 'family.'" Amber did not think it would be fair if she came out so soon after they did, so she chose to wait. "I was young, and I knew I could come out in college and I would have their full support."

Like Amber, many second generation children find college or other settings away from home to be opportunities to gain perspective on their own identity separate from their parents' identity.

ACROSS THE GENERATIONS

Since parents and children identify anywhere along a broad spectrum of lesbian, gay, bisexual, and transgender identities, there are endless combinations of second generation families. A lesbian daughter of politically active lesbian mothers, for example, will have a different second generation experience than a daughter raised by a closeted gay dad. Another family could include a transgender child and a gay dad. Another might have a bisexual mother with more than one queer son. Although "second generation" is an umbrella term for all LGBT kids with LGBT parents, there is no definitive second generation family experience that represents them all.

Fin, 24, was already a teenager when she realized most people used biological sex as a major criterion for whom they love. Fin, who identifies as pansexual and nongendered, was parented primarily by her grandmother, who is bisexual. "My grandmother just never seemed to care what the sex was of the person she loved," Fin says, "and that seemed natural to me." She explains how growing up with an openly bisexual grandmother made her coming-out experience different from that of queer people raised by heterosexual parents:

I've never had that difficult coming-out experience everyone talks about. Being as I am seems natural, and it's how I thought everyone was for most of my life. I think I was probably as I am more or less from birth, and I just had an easier time accepting that because of my environment. I have no shame related to sexual orientation or gender issues. I think I had a significantly less stressful adolescence because of it.

Evan, 22, also says that being second generation made coming out less stressful for him. He remembers how, when he was in college, his mother and her partner asked if he was "seeing anyone":

I took a great big breath and decided it was best not to lie. So I slyly slipped in the male pronoun and said, "Why, yes, actually I am seeing someone. And he's wonderful." I will never forget the look on their faces; kind of dumbfounded, you know. They said, "Does this mean what we think it means?" I just nodded. My stepmother—who has been out some twenty-odd years—looked at me and said, "Make sure it's the truth, because it is hard as hell to go back if it isn't." That was pretty much the conversation. I finished telling them about my boyfriend.

Evan's parents were surprised by his news only because the last they had known, he had been in a relationship with a woman for several months. Even though Evan's parents were supportive when he told them, he appreciated their follow-up phone call a few days later to reassure him that he had their support. "There wasn't the guilt and stuff that comes along with being the outcast in the family," Evan says. "I feel very close and connected to my family, different though it may be." When LGBT parents are prepared for the possibility of their kids coming out, they can alleviate the common anxiety that many of these children feel of disappointing their parents.

Beyond coming out, queer children and their LGBT parents don't always see eye to eye on LGBT issues, especially with identity politics evolving so rapidly over the past several decades. The issues caught in the queer generation gap include how open someone should be about their sexuality and how involved LGBT people should be in activism. Some parents see their children's openness as too "in your face" and would prefer them to be more discreet. What the parents consider as discretion, the children view as upholding shame.

Rachel, 32, grew up with a closeted bisexual mom who did not approve of Rachel being public about her own bisexuality. She has since gained perspective on the era in which her parents grew up and its influence on their feelings about how their daughter should conduct herself:

> I understand the generational thing better. And they have grown, too. Recently they were at dinner with another couple, and one of the people said something homophobic, and Dad said, "I have a bisexual daughter and I don't appreciate that remark." And then Mom added, "And a bisexual wife!" and stormed out. Wow, was I proud.

Other generational conflicts between parents and children in LGBT communities involve differing ideas about language and identity. "I am comfortable identifying as a lesbian, as bi, or as queer," Les explains. "I understand, though, that my mother's word for herself is 'gay,' and that many people of her generation will not identify as 'queer.'"

Parents who think the only ways for people to identify are "gay" or "straight" have a difficult time understanding what it means when a child comes out as bisexual. Biphobia still exists in lesbian and gay communities, and it is even more common for older gay people to say they "don't believe" in bisexuality. Transphobia is also more prevalent among people from older generations, causing conflicts with queer children who embrace gender fluidity for themselves and for others.

Children's acceptance of fluid identities can be especially confusing to parents when a child identifies simply as "queer" but will not claim any label beyond that. This can cause frustration between them, as the queer child wants to be accepted just as he or she is, and the parent keeps asking, "Okay! But *what* are you?"

AJ Turpen Fried was born biologically female, but at twenty he came out as transgender. That's when AJ, now twenty-six, learned that his father, whom AJ had understood to be gay, actually identifies as transgender as well. AJ says that his dad had been living as a gay man rather than coming out as transgender because of his strict notion of gender. AJ explains:

> Transpeople of his generation have a very different idea of what it means to be male or female. Like with my dad, it is all or nothing. He's chosen for a good twenty years to live in an identity he didn't identify with because he has always felt that in order to be a woman, he would have to go all the way. He has a fifties mentality of what it means to be a woman, like wearing a dress every day. I struggle about his coming out [as transgender] with those attitudes.

AJ's idea of what it is to be transgender is less rigid than his father's. AJ thinks that "if someone says they're transgender, then they're transgender." Unlike his father, AJ and his partner, who is also transgender, don't feel the need to physically transition in order to have their identities validated. He continues:

> I feel like even if I transition my entire body, I'm still going to be me. Someday I might make those choices [to take hormones or have surgery], but even if I do all those things, I'm always going to be a different kind of guy. I have a female history. My dad is judgmental about that, and about other trans-

gender people; that they're not *doing* enough. He thinks you should *do* more to pass. . . . My partner and I identify very differently [from my father]. I ask people around me to use male pronouns, but I don't necessarily do anything to pass.

While the generation gaps make some people on either side of the age spectrum judgmental about differences, second generation children enter adulthood benefiting from a broad perspective on queer ideology and history that spans several decades. Their awareness of queer culture often began years before they came out themselves.

"I was always reading books with gay characters," Greta explains, "and listening to music by gay artists. I knew the lingo before joining [the LGBT organization on campus] or even thinking about my own sexuality. . . . I do not think it was just 'questioning' curiosity. As the daughter of a lesbian, the gay community was a place where I fit in. . . . My opinions were appreciated and often sought after in the gay community, as an activist."

Second generation children feel a deep connection to the struggle for liberation through the years, something they often see queer people their own age take for granted. "I have a better sense of LGBT history," comments Les, "and what it was like for same-sex couples to meet and partner at a time when gay bars didn't exist. Or if they did, you could get fired from your job for going to one." Les adds that like many people who are second generation, she enjoys intergenerational friendships in a community that often divides itself by age groups.

Although society is far from achieving full equality, having a more historical perspective makes Evan grateful for the progress of queer liberation:

I have not grown up in the thirties or even the sixties and seventies when it was so very hard for people to come out. I am one in like five million young homosexuals that come out every year. It just doesn't seem so hard for us anymore. I mean, yes, there is hatred and there are hate crimes, and it is just not easy to be of a different sexual orientation. Yes, it is hard, but look at what we have to go through and compare it to what so many others have had to go through.

While young LGBT people who have straight parents may view older LGBT generations as outdated or conservative, children of LGBT parents are often less judgmental. Those who are second generation have a sense of history that gives them more patience and empathy for the older generations—even when they do not always agree with their ideology.

COMING OUT TO CLOSETED PARENTS

Although some second generation children feel fortunate to come out to supportive parents, this does not mean that coming out is always an effortless process. They still face concerns about reactions from their extended family, friends, school, and work. Additionally, second generation children are not always coming out to a parent who is *openly* gay. Sometimes a parent comes out *after* the child, rather than the other way around. And sometimes the parent never really comes out at all.

Jennifer Hubbard, 36, who is raising two children with her partner, grew up with her mom and her mom's partner, although little was acknowledged about the same-sex relationship. When Jennifer came out as lesbian, her mother was not supportive, making it difficult for Jennifer to accept herself. "My mom didn't like the idea," Jennifer says. "She still doesn't believe she is gay. I think that I spent way too many years trying to prove to myself that I was straight. It made me stay in a bad heterosexual relationship way too long."

Even though it was not discussed extensively, when Jennifer came out she already knew about her mother's sexuality. Other children think they are coming out to a straight parent, but later learn the parent was closeted. When parents are closeted, their lack of support for their queer children echoes their own reasons for not choosing to live openly gay: *Your life will be so difficult. You will never have children. You could live the straight lifestyle if you tried hard enough.* With their own fears preventing them from being open, some parents resent their children for having the courage they themselves lacked. Additionally, some parents fear that regardless of how hard they have tried to live as heterosexual people, their sexuality still "made" their children queer.

Jessi Hempel, 27, came out to her mother and father—who were still married at the time—when she was nineteen. The fact that her dad was hiding his sexuality added to the tension and isolation of her own coming-out experience. "When I first came out, I was very nervous," Jessi remembers. "I had had no exposure to gayness in any way. I sort of thought I was dying. I had this plan that if it was true that I was gay, I was going to have to move away and make new friends."

When Jessi told her parents, her mother cried, saying she had always known, but then suggested that it was a phase. Jessi's father said nothing. Later, a somewhat cryptic conversation with her father explained his silence. "My dad said, 'You know, I thought I was gay once, too,'" Jessi recalls. "There was this awkward pause, and then he said, 'You make choices in your life, and I chose to marry your mom.'"

Her father's pseudo-disclosure confirmed that coming out was the right decision for her. "At that moment," says Jessi, "I knew that my dad could have ended up like me. At the same time I was thinking, maybe I could end up like him."

Since Jessi is gay, most people assume she was immediately accepting of her dad when he came out, but other issues made it difficult to support him. Her father did not come out by choice, but was eventually forced out of the closet when his family discovered evidence of his on-line affairs. He was coming to terms with his own shame while at the same time turning to Jessi for support, as she explains:

> He sought me out as the other gay one [in the family because he thought] of course I would understand. He'd say, "There are unhealthy ways of expressing my sexuality." The message that came out of that for me was homosexuality is unhealthy, and I'm like, "Okay, but I'm a *healthy* homosexual." So how do I contextualize my experience of being gay when my dad thinks it's unhealthy? I couldn't support him. I couldn't help him out of the closet in any way, shape, or form. I moved to California. I really needed my distance.

Rachel also had mixed feelings when her mother came out, but for different reasons. The three years between Rachel's coming-out and her mother's were particularly difficult for Rachel. Finding out that her mother was bisexual made her "doubly mad" about how her parents had dealt with her own coming-out process:

> I was welcoming when Mom told me her orientation, but also I held back on expressing my anger. Why anger? My parents supported my liking other women but were harsh in trying to force me to stay in the closet to all people but my lovers. They actually threatened to kick me out a couple of times when I wanted to join campus queer clubs or march at Pride. So early on it was pretty much like coming out to straight parents, and you can see why I felt angry when Mom did come out.

Rachel had not had contact with her parents for a couple years, which left her financially unable to continue college. When they reconciled, her parents helped her return to school. "I pretty much made it clear then," she explains, "that they needed to accept it, or not have a daughter. They chose the daughter." She has since earned a Ph.D. and continues to live openly in all aspects of her life.

For Jessi, her emotional distance from her father was also temporary. She and her father carefully built a new relationship over a number of years. She says that her father—who once saw himself as "unhealthy"—has "evolved into this really hip, cool gay guy."

When a parent comes out to an openly queer child, there is no guarantee that the experience will cause the two to bond. Sons and daughters can find it jarring when a parent comes out and starts sharing personal information as if they are best friends rather than a grown child and a parent. Parents need to remember that children do not want to hear about a gay parent's sex life any more than they did when they thought the parent was straight. It's important that parents maintain parent-child boundaries, rather than depending on their queer children to be their sounding boards, de facto therapists, and "tour guides" into the LGBT community.

Parents who come out after a child need to be patient if their children are not immediately accepting of the news. This is especially true if the closeted parent reacted in a homophobic way when the child came out. Children's resentment toward newly out parents is exacerbated when parents seem to have selective memory and convince themselves that they have always been queer-supportive. The first step a parent can make to help dissolve that resentment is an apology, acknowledging their regret for making the child's coming-out process more difficult than it had to be.

COMING OUT TO A STRAIGHT PARENT

Children initially raised in a heterosexual marriage in which one of the parents eventually came out have the added dynamic of coming out to the parent who is straight. This can be a particularly difficult situation if the straight parent is still upset by the divorce or expresses negative opinions about gay people in general. A straight spouse might also see a child's coming-out as an act of betrayal or taking sides. It may bring up unresolved feelings of deceit and desertion. Such powerful feelings can bring on extreme reactions. Danna Cook, 18, talked to her mother, who is straight, about her feelings after Danna's sister came out. "My mother felt very betrayed," Danna says, "like my sister being a lesbian was somehow her taking our [gay] father's side or something." She asked her mother how she would react if Danna also came out. "Her response was partly joking," Danna says, "but with serious desperation. She said 'If you were a lesbian, I'd kill myself.'"

Her mother soon apologized and said she would support Danna if she came out, but that she would also be very sad. Danna understands that her mother was going through a difficult adjustment with her sister's coming-out, but she also says her mother's reaction put "unfair pressure" on her. "Being the daughter of a gay parent," Danna explains, "you question your sexuality sooner and more than most adolescents. . . . I consider myself straight, and even if I continued to be so forever, I still thought it wasn't right for her to give me any sort of constraints on who I am with such a severe threat of suicide."

While most straight spouses probably will not articulate their fears so explicitly, they might still send unintentional messages that cause kids anxiety about their sexual identity. A number of years ago I spoke on a panel for a therapists' association. Included on the panel was a heterosexual mother who was co-parenting her eleven-year-old son with her former husband, who had come out as gay. When she spoke, she explained how her husband's sexual orientation initially made her worry that their son would also be gay. She eventually stopped being preoccupied about her pre-adolescent's sexuality, when she was "relieved to find him showing an interest in girls." She smiled and nodded at her son, who sank into his chair. Deliberate or not, this mother told her son in a very public way that she wanted him to be heterosexual.

If the straight parents remain neutral about their children's emerging sexual identities, they can be wonderful allies for children who do come out. "I was amazed at the response I got from my [heterosexual] mom," Sarah says. "She was so excited and proud of me. Even though it took her a long time to get over the hurt of my father leaving the marriage, she was always supportive of him and of me." A straight parent has already watched the coming-out process in the midst of marital crisis. This time around, straight parents who support their second generation children offer insight, wisdom, and empathy that can make a tremendous difference in how their children feel about themselves.

SUPPORTING SECOND GENERATION CHILDREN

The stigma attached to being second generation must end on all levels: in broader society, in LGBT communities, in LGBT family circles, and in individual LGBT families. LGBT parents can begin to lessen that stigma by making sure their children know that heterosexuality needn't be either automatic or absolute for children of LGBT parents. That way, if their children are questioning their sexuality, they can be reassured that the politics around this issue will not extend to their home. Parents can also prepare friends and relatives—even before the children are born—letting them know that there's no guarantee whether the kids will grow up straight or gay, and that each one will be supported no matter what. Getting relatives used to the idea early on will minimize the drama should a child later come out.

Individuals in LGBT communities need to remind one another to avoid any comments that reveal a preference for their kids being heterosexual, even if the comments are well intended. Either because of their internalized homophobia or because of the hardships they endured, LGBT parents sometimes tell their children that they hope they turn out straight. "My parents were concerned that we had good lives," says Jessi, "and if my parents had to choose, they would prefer that we were straight rather than gay. It was directly said. I don't think my dad would say that anymore. Just over the past year he's changed his perspective on that."

Regardless of how parents feel, expressing hope that their children be straight will not improve the situation for children who are questioning their sexuality. A parent's preference about a child's sexuality does not influence a child's sexual orientation; it influences only how a child feels about coming out. In Jessi's case, the comments were specifically directed to her. More often, however, parents make offhand negative comments that they don't even realize their children overhear and internalize. Dan remembers as a teenager hearing his closeted mom talk to her friends about common acquaintances and noting when someone "unfortunately turned out to be gay."

Debra also understood implied messages in one of her mother's "random comments":

> When she was talking about her own life . . . she'd say, "It's hard to be gay and be a gay parent, and to get other people to accept your family." That was just something that influenced me. It told me that being straight would be better. That wasn't the impression she was trying to give me. She was just talking about her own life. She didn't mean [for her comments] to influence me, but [they] did.

Parents who worry about their children being gay neglect to see the ways in which having queer parents can be an advantage to a child who is coming out. Openly LGBT parents and their friends serve as role models for these children and help them learn strategies for dealing with homophobia. If their parents are out, second generation children grow up understanding that homosexuality is not wrong or sinful, and as a result have less internalized homophobia. In contrast, queer youth with straight parents have to make a concerted effort to meet LGBT people and learn that being gay is really not the deviant, abnormal lifestyle that society has led them to believe it is. Additionally, people who are second generation grow up already knowing that parenthood is a choice available to them. This seems obvious to them, but many of their peers with straight parents still believe coming out means having to let go of their dreams of having children.

Children with LGBT parents who begin to question their sexuality can explore that identity with an increased self-awareness and a sense of pride. Understanding sexuality in the context of identity, rather than simply behavior, shows questioning children that it is not sexual acts that "make" someone queer. This means that identifying with a particular orientation does not require being sexually active if they are not interested or ready. Having more positive perspectives on what it is to be queer can also help sons and daughters avoid self-destructive behaviors that stem from doubt and self-loathing, such as drug abuse and suicide.

For parents who are beginning to see hints of queerness in their children, it is helpful to keep the channels of communication open. However, no child needs to be pushed to "decide." When children feel pressure to identify their sexuality much more publicly and definitively than children of straight parents, they are denied the chance to figure it out in their own time. Expecting children to verbally define their sexuality also ignores the possibility that some children are content to remain ambiguous, and should not be expected to claim any particular identity—ever—if they don't personally find it necessary.

When we assess the outcomes of LGBT parenting, the answer to whether the kids are gay or straight should not matter. There are more important questions to address: Are these children fulfilled in their lives? Are they making life decisions wisely? Are they able to build healthy relationships? The answers to these questions are what will truly give insight into the "success" of LGBT parenting.

While the underlying fear is that LGBT parents will be judged harshly by homo-hostile people if their children come out, the reality is that queer families are judged harshly regardless. When parents focus on supporting their children, and are not preoccupied with what outsiders think, they draw from their own life experience to provide a less judgmental coming-out process. LGBT parents who disregard the politics have the opportunity to pass on a priceless gift to their second generation children: pride in discovering their authentic selves.

Eight

Tourists at Home: Straight Kids in Queer Culture

The gay community and the gay culture, I grew up in that. To think that that's not a part of who I am or who I have become would be denial.

—ORSON MORRISON, 30

While I was browsing in the local feminist bookstore, I bumped into the mother of a boy I had met a few years earlier. It is not unusual for me to see people I know there, because as happens in many cities, this bookstore serves as a de facto queer community center. I asked this mother about her son, as I had not seen him in more than a year. He used to be secretive about his mother being lesbian and about her partner, but after meeting kids in similar families, he started to become more open. She told me that her son had bravely faced seventh grade, and after spending fifth and sixth grade wondering how people would treat him if they knew he had lesbian parents, he was now one of the leaders of his school's gay-straight alliance. "He's so comfortable now," she told me, her eyes sparkling. "This bookstore has been a great resource for him. He loves coming with me so that he can check out gay and lesbian films for his GSA."

Her comment made me wonder how the employees and customers will react in a few years when he drives to the bookstore without his mother accompanying him to explain his connection. Right now he is a cute and harmless twelve-year-old, but soon he will be a man; someone whom unknowing customers might feel is invading their "safe space." Yet as homophobia increases during the teen years, this young man will likely turn to that bookstore as his refuge as much, if not more, than he did when he was a little boy—even if he turns out to be heterosexual. Will he always feel welcome there?

Children who are being raised by openly LGBT parents and then "come out" as heterosexual bring some challenging questions to discussions about identity and community. What happens when straight adult children want to integrate into a community that defines "safe space" as the absence of heterosexuals? How do straight sons and daughters raised in predominantly queer settings adjust to living in predominantly straight settings once they are grown? How can straight children be raised to be proud of their families without being ashamed of their own—but different—sexuality?

People think I'm joking when I pose these kinds of questions, but I'm not. These questions go beyond the basics of how LGBT people can become parents, or what rights they do or do not have to raise children. They look into issues deeper than the common questions about how the kids "turn out" or how they identify sexually. These are long-term questions that address how children of LGBT parents will challenge and shape mainstream cultures and queer cultures—two worlds that have operated most comfortably independent of each other.

WHAT IS QUEER CULTURE?

Studying anthropology in college, my classmates and I were frequently challenged to define "culture." It is a word used constantly in the discipline, and I spent much of my time examining various scholarly interpretations of its meaning. Culture can be more clearly understood not by pinning down an official definition, but by comparing how one particular culture is different from another. For example, when I read about an isolated tribe on an island on the other side of the world, I saw that it was easy to describe their culture. Their clothing, language, food, celebrations, and traditions were all different from mine, thus leading me to conclude that the tribe had a "rich culture." Yet if one of the tribal members who had never left the island were asked about his culture, he might not even understand the concept.

To insiders, the environment in which they are raised is not "culture." It simply *is*. Individuals immersed in a community do not become cognizant of their common culture until they come into contact with another community that is different from theirs. It is then that they can identify and understand the specifics of the culture in which they are operating.

Even though culture is not always articulated, each individual is shaped and influenced by the cultural context in which he or she is raised. That context creates a collective frame of reference that includes shared values, belief systems, and history. From this abstract frame of reference, concrete cultural factors emerge, such as customs, music, literature, dance, and language. Many sons and daughters of LGBT parents—the majority of whom turn out to be heterosexual—enter adulthood with strong connections to their queer cultural heritage.

Some aspects in queer culture are expressions of celebration and pride, like the rainbow flag and community gatherings. Others, such as coded language and symbols, were created out of the necessity to safely communicate with other LGBT people without straight people noticing. As more communities become gay-friendly, the need to remain secretive becomes less necessary for survival, yet the cultural factors remain.

For example, "family" is a word commonly used to indicate someone is gay. Once, when I needed to hire a sign-language interpreter, I called a woman who signs regularly at several LGBT events. She was unavailable for the specific date, so I asked her to recommend someone else. As she scanned her list of colleagues, she said, "I assume you want someone who is family." She could have safely said "LGBT" or "queer" instead of "family," but even when there is no threat present, using code establishes a level of familiarity that affirms our connection to one another through our shared culture.

Homo-hostile people are quick to dismiss the assertion that queerness creates a legitimate culture, asserting that same-sex sexual orientation is simply behavior, not identity. Some LGBT people are also resistant to the idea, insisting that the only thing that connects them to the LGBT community is their sexual desire or gender identity. It is indeed their sexuality that makes them identify as lesbian, gay, bisexual, or transgender, but the common ground that creates LGBT communities is not just sex. As a result of being part of a population that historically has been oppressed, ostracized, and ignored, LGBT people have necessarily participated in the emergence of alternatives to the dominant culture.

As a child in a gay family, I developed some sensibilities that made me identify strongly with the culture of gay men. Like the gay men I observed around me, I had strong "gaydar," which made it possible to spot gay men in public. I went to Twin Cities Gay Men's Chorus concerts to lift my spirits, I regularly read the gay newspapers, and I developed daily strategies to live with pride in an overwhelmingly homo-hostile world. Identifying with this culture gave me a sense of belonging I took for granted as a child. It was like breathing oxygen—I didn't really notice how vital it was to my life until I no longer had access to it.

When I entered my first year at a women's college, I was abruptly cut off from connections to my upbringing. What I missed most was being in public with Dad and Russ and feeling a special connection to gay strangers. I felt like I spoke a telepathic language with gay people, and I found comfort in making meaningful eye contact with them to establish an unspoken mutual understanding: "You're gay, my dads are gay. I'm on your side."

I knew logically that not all heterosexuals warranted a feeling of suspicion, but when it came to strangers, my ongoing fear of falling into a threatening situation made me assume anyone was a homophobe until proven otherwise. In this new setting, with women my age instead of older men who knew my family history, I was annoyed and saddened to realize that I was indistinguishable from any other heterosexual. I convinced myself that the lesbian and bisexual organizers on campus were judgmental of me, assuming I was a homophobe or, at best, a clueless "het." A few times I considered telling some of the openly lesbian students why I was not as clueless as they might think. I decided against it because it seemed silly to defend myself that way, especially when I did not even understand what I was looking for. What did my dad's sexuality have to do with me? And why did I want access to their community, anyway?

Getting some perspective by being away from my family made me realize how much I had considered the gay community to be *my* community, and gay rights to be *my* struggle as much as my parents' struggle. For as long as I could remember, I had viewed "those straight people" as the ones who made my family life more difficult than it had to be. "Those straight people" included the politicians who passed laws that conflated religious beliefs with human rights. "Those straight people" included the teens who yelled "faggot" at my father's house when they drove by. To ultimately come out as heterosexual—by default becoming one of "those straight people"—felt like an act of treason. Yet I also knew I did not fit into the gay community like I used to. Since I no longer walked into queer environments with Dad or Russ as my passport, I was a suspicious outsider—a tourist at home.

Although I am a woman who is attracted to men, simply saying I am heterosexual wipes away my history and dismisses the pride I have in my heritage. Many adult children in LGBT families explain that while they have no feelings of same-sex attraction, they are still hesitant to identify openly as heterosexual for fear of being excluded from their familiar social networks. They do not want to be associated with the queer stereotypes of heterosexuals—that they are close-minded, that they contribute to a system of oppression, and that they are oblivious to their privilege. As one daughter says, "I have an issue with being seen as straight. What frustrates me is just being placed in a category and having that be the end. That closes a door of possibility in the queer community's eyes. I think that goes back to me wanting to be recognized for still being part of the community."

My own ambivalence about heterosexuality made me wonder whether this was what was meant by the antigay rhetoric about children of gay parents being confused. Then, when I was twenty-six, I heard the words that made everything make more sense: "culturally queer, erotically straight." Stefan Lynch, 31, the first director of CO-LAGE, invented the term to describe the bicultural identity of heterosexual children who are linked to queerness through their heritage. Up to that point, my only interaction with kids of gay and lesbian parents had been with teenagers, not adult children. Since cultural queerness becomes most apparent with the onset of adulthood, the teens were not yet verbalizing what I had been experiencing. Alone, I tried to ignore my nagging feelings of emotional exile. But after learning that my sense of identity was shared with a larger population, I stopped thinking of my longing as mere intellectual whining. Now that I had a way to talk about it, I realized that it wasn't whining; it was homesickness.

Like other children raised in queer communities, Jesse Gilbert, 30, began to ask himself questions when he was a teenager. "Where do I fit in here?" he began to wonder. "Where am I in this community as I grow up? If you reject it, you're messed up, and if you embrace it, you're criticized. Damned if you do, and damned if you don't. It's a no-win scenario."

Jesse says the no-win scenario is a result of the contradictory message parents give their children with the onset of adulthood. Since birth, children are celebrated for being part of the queer community, even encouraged to participate as activists. But as the children grow up, LGBT people—including their parents—are surprised when they want to stay involved even if they are straight. The assumption is that straight adult children belong in the straight "mainstream" community. At the same time, however, these same children are often viewed as outsiders to the mainstream. Because they have been "queered" by their upbringing, their sensibilities set off cues that they're not quite like other straight people, placing these children in a cultural limbo.

"I think that it's hard for both the queer community and the straight community to know what to do with us," says Orson, who is heterosexual. "What are we part of? Are we part of the queer community? Are we part of the straight community? . . . I think that maybe it's a little easier for second generation people to feel welcomed into the community."

Many children first express their cultural queerness when they are very young, but in simple terms that parents misinterpret. Children as young as four or five say things like, "My dads are gay and so am I." Before parents panic about being accused of "recruiting" their young children, it is important to consider what a five-year-old could mean when she says she is gay. It could be that she is not really gay, but simply expressing pride in her family and heritage. At that young age, "gay identity" and "gay culture" are terms that are too abstract for them to articulate. The questions about their own sexual identities will ultimately resolve themselves as the children mature, but the questions surrounding cultural identity remain.

DIVERSITY WITHIN QUEER CULTURE

Ask ten sons and daughters what makes them "culturally queer" and each will have a different explanation. Many factors contribute to how children with LGBT parents are "queered." Referring to "the LGBT community" actually refers to a collection of numerous communities. There are gay communities, lesbian communities, bisexual communities, and transgender communities. Within each of these communities is a broad spectrum of experiences and perspectives.

Without a universal queer culture, children's frame of reference will be influenced by many factors, including their own families, hometown, and the time period in which they grew up. Children with lesbian parents in a rural area in the Midwest, for example, have a frame of reference that is markedly different from children with gay male parents in an urban setting on the West Coast. Families' racial background, their socioeconomic status, the degree to which they are out, and their access to LGBT community events all contribute to shaping the queer lens through which these children see their world.

"I know much more about window treatments, Judy Garland, and fresh-cut flowers than other straight guys," says Topher Connors, 30, whose father is gay. Meema Spadola, 33, who has a lesbian mother, recognizes significant differences between the queer culture she knows and the one that children of gay male parents experience. Meema says, "Growing up in Maine among hearty, cabin-building, wood-chopping potluck-dinner-giving lesbians, I exist in a completely different world."

Since variations of queer culture are also marked by generational differences, straight children often feel more connected to gay and lesbian people from their parents' generation than to queer people their own age. Ari, 28, who has a lesbian mom, says he feels camaraderie with older lesbians, even if they do not initially pick up on it. In his effort to make sure lesbians understand that he is queer-friendly, Ari lets them know his mother is lesbian without specifically saying it—to do so would break the cultural rule of coded language among older lesbians. He says, "I just tell them that my mother is 'studying women's history.' They figure it out from that."

Despite the diversity in cultural queerness, important commonalities emerge among children of LGBT parents. Kate Ranson-Walsh, 23, a second generation COLAGEr who has been involved with the organization for more than half of her life, explains:

> The queer community *is* its own culture and the queer community isn't just about who you have sex with or who you are attracted to. The culture, of course, is also multifaceted . . . maybe [colagers] *do* exist in different cultures, but the commonality that brings us all together is that our culture is different or deviant from the norm culture. That is our joined culture. And almost every person I've met who comes from this background feels some sort of bond and connection to other people in this position.

Most parents who are focused on raising their children while immersed in queer culture don't have the time or the inclination to think about the larger questions I am raising. When I first ask them about what parts of their experience might "queer" their children, the question seems unanswerable. After I offer some examples, parents begin to catch on to the concept, and they enjoy seeing their queerness from a different perspective. Parents make the connection between identity exploration and their children choosing college majors such as anthropology, sociology, psychology, and gender studies. Lesbian mothers chuckle when they realize how their culture has inspired their teen's skill at planning potluck dinners with his fellow social-change activists. A gay father starts to understand why his daughter dreams of becoming a torch singer. What seemed like unusual choices or behavior in their children begin to make more sense once parents can see how queer culture is influencing their children.

LONGING FOR HOME

By choice and by habit, culturally queer adults feel a special connection with LGBT people and are drawn to places that reflect their heritage, such as coffeehouses, bars, and community gatherings like Pride. Jenny Laden, 32, describes how, as a straight woman, she still feels connected to gay men:

> I get along with gay men incredibly well, because I get them. In many ways I'm like them because I was raised by a gay man. . . . Gay men are such an intrinsic part of who I am, from humor to tastes to attitude. I love fabulousness. And my comfort with that culture has only been reinforced by spending lots of time with my friends who are gay men.

Yet, when they are grown, heterosexual children discover that they do not fit into their community as they used to. As the only child of a single gay dad in Haight-Ashbury, Alysia Abbott, 32, noticed this shift:

> Growing up, I was the only girl around all these men, and that afforded me a special place that I enjoyed. . . . I had this idea that I could always go to neighborhoods like the Castro [in San Francisco] and Christopher Street [in New York City] where I could be with "my people." There would be cafés and bars, and I could meet up with old friends. But when I became an adult and my father was no longer living, I didn't have any

entry into it. I found out that it was his community, not mine. I wish I were more connected now. That is something that I long for.

Alysia refers to this longing as "genvy"—a combination of "gay" and "envy." "I want to be part of the community," explains Alysia. "I want to say, 'Hey, I have this connection.' On some occasions, if I am with a group of gay men, I'll let them know my dad was gay. It gives me a kind of 'in' with some gay men."

Like Alysia, daughters with gay dads and sons with lesbian mothers also challenge community boundaries that are defined not only by sexual orientation but also by gender. Many adult children speak fondly of being the only girl in male space, or the only boy in lesbian space. They loved feeling special, and getting a lot of attention. As Jesse remembers:

> I spent the vast majority of time with women. They weren't exactly separatists, but they were pretty radical. So they didn't even know that many gay men. They were interested in being in a non-male space. I was always the exception. . . . I used to go to these lesbian feminist fundraisers and I would be the only male. It was actually fun for me because I was special. And everyone knew who I was because I was the only boy. . . . There may have been one or two times when someone said, "Why is *he* here?" And they'd say, "He's here because we're here. He's here because he's welcome here."

As boys mature, women are less tolerant of mothers wanting their sons to be the exception in women-only space. The Michigan Womyn's Music Festival is a striking example of how boys receive mixed messages as they grow up. As an annual women-only event, the Festival offers children's programming for daughters of all ages. Sons are also welcome, but only up to age ten. When the boys turn eleven, they are excluded because of something that is out of their control: becoming men. While intellectually, boys are able to respect women-only space, it can be distressing to them to be excluded. Arthur Elliott, 29, explains:

> I was thirteen when they started going to [the] Michigan Womyn's Festival. I couldn't go. I understood the reasoning for women-only space because that was how I was raised. I was always raised by my mom to see their viewpoint of culture and how it is male-dominated. But I still resented it; it kind of sucked for me. I did tell them that I thought it wasn't really fair that I couldn't go just because of my age. Rules are rules, but I should have been an exception.

It was confusing and frustrating for Arthur, who didn't identify with much of what his gender symbolized in women-only communities. After all, he helped run the family's feminist bookstore and had been harassed by boys at school because of his family. He did not want to accept an automatic affiliation with the much-maligned patriarchal system simply because of his age and gender.

Overall, straight sons are viewed as more unusual or suspect than straight daughters when they choose to be in queer settings. Straight women have traditionally socialized with both lesbians and gay men, while straight men have not. Although there have been historical tensions between lesbians and heterosexual feminists, they continue to share common ground and political overlap in the fight against sexism. Straight women who socialize with gay men are common enough to warrant a slang term: "fag hags." I have yet to meet a daughter who appreciates that label, but at least the presence of women in gay male space is not perceived as all that unusual. There is little precedent in queer culture, however, for the presence of straight men, without their intentions being questioned. If straight sons want to socialize with lesbians, they are assumed to be a threat. And if straight sons choose to be in gay male space, they are assumed to be in denial about being gay.

Because of the sensibilities Aaron developed as he grew up in a lesbian household, he doesn't like putting up with the homophobia that is so prevalent when he plays on men's sports teams. Searching for an opportunity to participate in competitive sports free from anti-gay attitudes, he joined a gay rugby team. "A lot of [gay teammates] didn't really understand," says Aaron, 28. "They were like, 'Why are you playing on this team?' I'd say, 'Because I'm more comfortable here. I come from an alternative family.' And the guys were like, '*What?!*'"

Ultimately Aaron left the gay rugby team. He says they were losing anyway, but also that the after-game drinking parties were heavy with flirting. "I don't always enjoy being affectionate with men, and I kind of felt like I had to be to fit in," he explained. Aaron chose to go back to playing on a non-gay team, where he tolerates the homophobia and suspects there might be "one or two closeted guys." His current teammates do not know about his family, nor does he plan to tell them.

Aaron's experience is the kind of culture clash that straight adult children commonly encounter when they try to live a straight life within their queer framework. Aaron says that becoming an adult has made him realize the tensions that result from, as he puts it, "growing up gay":

> Like it or not, most of the world didn't grow up in a gay family. The truth is that how we learn how to be in the world is deeply affected by our family upbringing. This includes how to relate to others, and what's "normal" behavior. The reality is that sometimes not having "normal" views or a "normal" upbringing can affect one negatively. Whether it comes to dating, playing on sports teams, whatever. Bottom line: We live in a straight world. Growing up gay doesn't always prepare you for that.

Living in cultural limbo is difficult at times. This does not mean that parents need to keep their queer identity separate from family life, assuming their children will then be able to adapt effortlessly to the dominant culture. Most of the time, the vibrancy of queer culture outweighs the frustration of cultural clashes. It is helpful to the children, however, for parents to be conscious of their culture's influence, because ignoring or denying it only adds to their children's frustrations. Parents can start exploring how queer culture influences their children specifically by referring to Appendix A, "Queer Cultural Brainstorm."

PASSING:
WHEN STRAIGHT KIDS ARE PRESUMED TO BE LGBT

There needs to be broader definition of community in queer circles in order to include sons and daughters, straight or not. To some people, this concept seems obvious; to others, it is threatening. One of the major justifications for keeping queer space exclusively LGBT is that straight people "just don't get it" or "don't understand." Queer-only space is where queer people can let down their guard and be themselves; therefore, when straight people enter that "safe space," it is no longer safe. The blanket assertion that children of LGBT parents would be a threat to queer safe space can be hurtful and insulting to the children, many of whom have sought out that same safe space for much of their lives. Jesse says that some LGBT people's refusal to consider straight children as community members is, in part, a denial of how these children are affected by homophobia:

It's like [LGBT people are saying]: "We have to deal with homophobia; *you* don't." But it's very possible that children have really interesting things to say about homophobia. Parents need to start acknowledging that, to say that actually, people growing up in these families do have something to say about it. It's a part of their life and a phenomenon they grew up with.

People in LGBT communities tend to ignore the impact of homophobia on children. After one of my lectures about culturally queer children, a woman who did not have children came up to me privately to deliver her oversimplified interpretation of my talk. "I take issue with what you say," she told me. "What's this 'I'm oppressed because I have a gay relative'? As a black lesbian, I do not have room for you in my struggle. If you are heterosexual, you will never know what it is like to fear getting the shit kicked out of you because of who is in your bed."

"That's right," I told her. "But I know what it is like to be six years old, fearing that my father—the person who was supposed to protect me—would get the shit kicked out of him because of who was in *his* bed."

Children of LGBT parents worry about their family's safety regardless of their own sexuality because hate crimes are still too common. One such assault occurred in 2003 at a public July Fourth celebration in Boston when a lesbian mother was with her partner and their two children. The victim says four teenagers taunted her family, laughed at them, and called them "dykes." In a confrontation later in the evening, the children, ages five and nine, watched as their mother was punched to the ground and kicked so brutally she suffered bleeding in her brain.[22]

As an adult, I also know what it is like to fear violence not because of who is in my bed, but because of who people *think* is in my bed. The connections that grown children have to LGBT communities are dismissed by people who, like the woman who confronted me, believe that heterosexual privilege automatically separates straight children from the communities that raised them. However, heterosexual privilege is based on perception. When homo-hostile people know our parents are gay, they often apply the "gay parents make gay babies" myth and assume that we, too, are gay. Additionally, grown children who are culturally queer unwittingly lead heterosexual people to perceive them as LGBT. Orson says that he is mistaken for gay "pretty regularly":

> I just think that part of me really identifies with gay male culture. My father is a fashion designer and hairstylist. I'm being very stereotypical right now, but that's the culture I grew up in. My uncle's a ballet dancer. I love fashion. I love the aesthetic. I love decorating my home. Those are the things that I saw growing up and what I have come to value. . . . I think that because I'm interested in LGBT issues and that I identify with it, people in the queer community often assume that I am gay, because why else would you be interested in it? They think I'm lying to myself.

Because heterosexual privilege is based on perception, straight yet queerly affiliated individuals like Orson risk forfeiting that privilege when they give cultural cues that suggest they are LGBT. While visiting a friend in San Francisco, I accompanied her and two other queer activists on a road trip to a nearby town. They were putting up posters to announce an upcoming LGBT gathering in the area. When we got out of the car on the main street, several people turned and stared. The car was decorated with bumper stickers with left-wing slogans, and my friend was wearing masculine clothing, including a tie. One of the women traveling with us looked up and down the street, assessing which direction would be less likely to provoke a confrontation.

"Okay," she said under her breath, "let's stick together and try not to get our asses kicked." We didn't run into any problems that day, but the fear was there. Had there been a confrontation, my heterosexuality would not have made me exempt from harassment. In the company of three queer women, I am also perceived to be queer, and gay bashers do not ask their victims to fill out a questionnaire before they strike. In 2002, ten percent of the reported victims of anti-LGBT violence identified as heterosexual.[23]

As a soldier in the National Guard, Topher says the "don't ask, don't tell" policy means that many people just assume he is gay. His gay sensibility, his refusal to join his fellow soldiers in homo-hostile banter, and frequenting a local gay bar make him as vulnerable to scrutiny as soldiers who actually *are* gay:

> Working for the army, I hear "fag" jokes constantly, and have put people in their place more than once. I am single, and everyone assumes I am gay, and I know for a fact that most everyone thinks I am a member of the "don't ask, don't tell" club. I swear I am going to be the only straight guy ever run out of the army for being gay.

Physical confrontations and professional discrimination are the more serious effects of homophobia that sons and daughters might face when they are assumed to be gay. Other consequences involve basic day-to-day hostility when interacting with strangers and acquaintances.

Sometimes when I think a stranger is reacting to me in a certain way because they are homophobic, I am not certain if I am being overly sensitive, reading too deeply into a reaction. I wonder, for example, when an airport baggage inspector gets cranky as she rummages through my carry-on stuffed with blatantly queer literature and buttons, is it because she thinks I'm gay? Or is she already having a bad day? When a bookstore employee doesn't make eye contact when I ask about a gay title, is it because he's homophobic? Or is he just shy? Rarely do I know for sure. One environment where reactions are very easy to interpret is on airplanes. In close quarters for several hours with no exit, you have to deal with the people around you, or at least be very obvious in your attempts *not* to deal with the people around you.

On a very full flight home from New York, I had a row of three seats to myself. As people were settling in, a teenage boy and girl who were assigned to the row behind me notified an airline attendant that they needed another place to sit. They had discovered that their seats had wet vomit on them from the previous flight. With apologies, the flight attendant moved the teenagers next to me. I buried my nose in a book, but before long, they were offering me some of their candy stash and telling me all about their spring break. When they asked me about my job, I told them, and the girl shrugged and said quickly, "That's cool." Then the boy said, "I don't have a problem with gays. But when they wanna, like, kiss and stuff in front of me, that's disgusting." I asked him whether he thought it was all right for his parents to kiss each other in public. He told me that of course that was fine. I told him that I wished someday my dad and his partner could kiss in public the way his mom and dad do without people thinking it was disgusting.

He didn't have a response, so I resumed reading my book. A few minutes later they both left the row. When more time passed than what it would have taken for them to stretch their legs, I was curious to see where they had gone. I craned my neck around to discover that they were sitting right behind me. They had draped a blanket over the seats to cover the vomit before they sat down. The seats next to me remained empty for the rest of the flight. In this situation, there was no room for misinterpretation. Such encounters demonstrate how being heterosexual does not make adult children of LGBT parents immune to homophobic reactions.

Sons and daughters are often assumed to be LGBT in queer settings, too. This assumption brings with it the challenge of deciding when it is appropriate to "come out" as heterosexual. Waiting too long can result in LGBT people feeling tricked or misled after they discover the truth, but bringing it up too soon comes off as defensive.

Mike Beebe, whose father is gay, wonders how to best clarify his sexuality when people assume he's gay. "I think I am read as gay because I have that sensitive-guy thing going on," says Mike, 33, "and I am an advocate for queer rights, so I must be gay, right? If I am interested in someone romantically and I want to make it clear that I am an eligible heterosexual guy, I have to find ways to come out as straight without coming off as homophobic."

Each time an LGBT person treats me differently after they discover that I am not gay, it reinforces the feeling that my sexual orientation pushes me across enemy lines. At LGBT conferences, I am often one of very few heterosexual people. During one of these conferences, I sat down for lunch at a table with a community leader whom I had gotten to know via e-mail over the previous year. As he was introducing me to the other people at the table, he put his hand on his chest and sat up straight like a proud parent bragging about his child making the honor roll.

"Abigail is second generation," he announced.

There are plenty of times when people presume I am second generation and the brevity of the interaction does not permit me to clarify. But when someone incorrectly declares my sexuality to other people, it seems like lying not to speak up.

"Actually, I'm not," I said that day at the conference. Everyone at the table froze.

"You're not?" My colleague's chest deflated. He had been sharing brainstorms and banter with me for nearly a year, all the while think-ing I was lesbian.

"I'm culturally queer. Queered by my upbringing of having gay parents." I had already lost his attention; he was scanning the room looking for someone, or pretending to look for someone. I knew he had a young daughter. I hope that by the time she is an adult, identify-ing as heterosexual does not evoke such dismissive reactions.

STRAIGHT SHAME

In my midtwenties I was talking with a friend who is bisexual, and I inadvertently mentioned a crush I had on a man. I immediately apolo-gized, drawing on politically correct language I had heard countless times. I told him I realized it wasn't appropriate for me to flaunt my heterosexual privilege, so I was going to keep quiet. He assured me that I shouldn't censor myself because my attractions happened to be to people of the opposite sex. He suggested I look at my "straight shame" and pointed out that I presented myself as an asexual person in LGBT settings, similar to the way closeted LGBT people present themselves in straight settings.

His comments made me think of how my father interacted with peo-ple in the church where he was a member for twenty years. He was not what homo-hesitant people would call "in your face"—he did not bring his partner to services and he never made any reference to his sexuality. It seemed that other church members accepted him as long as they did not have to be reminded he was gay. I thought of his church persona as Benign Homosexual; a toned-down version of the man I knew. I realized that in queer settings I was putting similar effort into avoiding criticism by not reminding anyone I was heterosexual. Until then, I was so used to being told to look at the privilege I had because I was heterosexual that I had not also considered the shame I might have about it.

In college, for instance, I brought a boyfriend to a Gay Men's Chorus concert because I wanted to share with him part of my life that was important to me. As we stood in the lobby at intermission, he put his arm around my waist. I loved it when my boyfriend showed affection, but in this setting, it made me wish I were invisible. I had grown up hearing gay men joke about watching the lone straight couple in gay settings, clinging to each other and going out of their way to make it clear that they were together. Now I loathed the idea that gay men would point me out as just another insecure "breeder."

Straight shame is not something parents set out to teach their children. Usually it takes the form of offhand comments about straight people that parents do not think children will hear. But just as second generation children internalize negative feelings about being gay, emerging straight children internalize negative feelings about being straight.

Stefan's gay father viewed heterosexual men as "boring at best, and hateful beasts at worst." His lesbian mother saw male sexuality as "uniformly fearful." Stefan internalized these ideas, which he says had a long-term effect on his feelings about his own sexuality:

> My mother's inability to [teach me to love myself as a man] and my dad's general distaste for heterosexuality shut me down because my sexuality was shameful. My acceptance of myself as a straight man didn't really occur until my midtwenties, when I had a fling with a woman who really reveled in my masculinity, male body, and sexuality. It was a phenomenal feeling, accompanied by a release of shame and guilt about my straight sexuality and male body that is ongoing.

Addressing a panel of teenagers of LGBT parents, one parent asked the kids what was particularly challenging about being in their families. Two of the teens voiced concern about what they called "heterophobia"—they wished their parents weren't so negative and distrusting of straight people. Even suggesting that heterophobia exists for these children understandably evokes angry and skeptical responses because homo-hostile people have used the same word to support a bogus claim that gay rights discriminate against heterosexuals. LGBT people argue that the world is saturated with heterosexual privilege, making heterophobia impossible. But for children, their "world" is the one their parents create around them. Heterophobia is not equal to homophobia in that it is not institutionalized discrimination and does not result in physical violence. From the children's perspective, however, heterophobia still exists in subtle ways that are tolerated in LGBT communities.

Heterophobic behavior includes cold receptions to people who are straight at LGBT community meetings, questioning the motives of heterosexual people who are outspoken about LGBT rights, and making dismissive comments about heterosexuals. ("That party had way too many breeders.") Some children believe their parents would prefer them to be something they are not: gay. Some parents distance themselves from their straight kids, who, to the parents, represent institutionalized heterosexism. Offhand misogynistic comments from gay dads or anti-male comments from lesbian mothers make children doubt whether their parents will accept them as men and women.

Even when comments are not explicit, kids can still interpret attitudes as demonstrating that heterosexuality is inferior. A few years ago, parents at an LGBT conference were touting conclusions from research on gay dads. The conclusions suggested that gay dads might have certain parenting skills that are stronger than those of straight dads. The fact that such research exists is not problematic, but talking smugly about it in front of children is. It did not seem to concern the parents that the oversimplified message of gay men being better dads than straight men would be internalized by their children, who might someday grow up to be straight parents.

STRAIGHT CHILDREN AND
THEIR ROMANTIC RELATIONSHIPS

As adults, culturally queer children bring their ideas about gender, sexuality, and queerness with them into relationships with the opposite sex. Their culture influences how they communicate with their partners and their perception of positive relationships. This can be confusing and frustrating because heterosexual relationships often assume more traditional ideas of gender roles. When they are not familiar with positive examples of heterosexual relationships, culturally queer children are challenged to sort through their preconceived notions of heterosexuality. These notions are the most distorted when kids are being raised in predominantly queer environments where they rarely encounter heterosexual people.

Ry Russo-Young, 22, is put off by the sexism and gender roles that she sees in heterosexual relationships. With her two mothers as her standard for what makes a positive relationship, she wonders whether she will find a relationship that is comparable:

> I grew up thinking I was a lesbian. . . . It took me a lot of struggle to realize that I really was attracted to men, yet now it is really hard for me to deal with men as human beings, let alone sexually. I know that I equate real love and equality [with] a gay relationship, and a less trustworthy, "dirty" sexualness to heterosexual relations. I see hetero sex everywhere in the media, and while intrigued, I am repulsed because I could never allow myself to fall into that sexist soul-losing domain of oppression. I cannot understand or relate to men because I am so immersed in gay culture and unfamiliar with what it is to have a healthy straight relationship.

Sons and daughters in heterosexual relationships are often surprised to encounter cultural clashes well into their adult years. For example, Arthur's communication style was frustrating to his girlfriend. Specifically, she was confused by Arthur's "processing," a common problem-solving practice in lesbian communities in which all ideas and feelings are shared. Arthur explains:

> I do like to process, and most of the guys that she has dated have been more controlling. I'm not, and that kind of aggravates my girlfriend; she'll say, "Be a man for a change!" I'm having to process a little bit less and she's having to process a little bit more. She brought it up first in a non-Southern way. She said something like, "You talk too much. You just gotta do more. I don't know if this is because of the way you were raised or what." It hurt at first, but of course, after I processed it, I saw she was right.

Understanding the differences in their communication styles because of the way each was raised helped Arthur and his girlfriend develop a new style of communication between them. Before they became aware of the reasons for these differences, they did not have the tools to adapt together. These sorts of conflicts often remain confusing and unresolved unless one member of a couple recognizes the need for a cultural translation.

For many heterosexual children, their queer sensibility includes a commitment to queer politics, and this can bring tension to their relationships. A boyfriend I dated soon after college became increasingly uneasy about my involvement in the LGBT community. While I had already suspected his growing discomfort, it became readily apparent after a local gay paper published an article about my activism. My boyfriend said, "I don't have a problem with you having a gay dad, but do you have to talk about it all the time?"

David Wells, 28, says a two-and-a-half-year relationship ended largely because of—as he describes it—his "roots." One Christmas

David was surprised that his girlfriend bought a wreath from the Boy Scouts. To David, buying and displaying the wreath in their home was a symbolic endorsement of the organization's exclusion of gay men. His girlfriend was not familiar with the issue or the Supreme Court ruling that allowed the discriminatory policy to stand. The next year a television program prompted a discussion between the couple about gay rights in which his girlfriend referred to certain gay activists as "extreme." As their discussion escalated into an argument, she revealed that she had again ordered a wreath from the Boy Scouts. David says the experience was "heart-wrenching":

> The actual wreath wasn't the problem. I was more shocked that someone who I loved and thought loved me and someone who I trusted would do that after she knew how much it affected me before. Something that you feel so passionately about—your family . . . not have that respected, I felt betrayed in my own home.

During their relationship, David's girlfriend seemed fine about his father on a personal level, but her perspective did not validate the link that David felt between his family and a bigger political struggle. "She was fairly supportive," David says, "but at the end of the day, she wasn't supportive enough. She just didn't get it."

For Darius Greenbacher, 32, his strong queer values influenced his feelings about heterosexual marriage. He had been with the same woman for several years. They had two dogs, owned a house together, and called one another their partner. In his partner's family, getting married was highly valued, so she was talking about marriage more frequently as they entered their late twenties. Darius's opposition to it began to cause serious problems in their relationship. "It was not that I didn't want to be her partner," Darius explains. "Most important was the feeling that I would betray my mom and Judy if I were to get married. I felt resentful that the institution of marriage would not accept my mom and Judy, my role models for relationships."

Darius and his partner had "many huge arguments" about marriage, but they found "no common ground." When Darius's partner left the country for the summer, both had some time apart for soul-searching. During that time, Darius's mother and her partner, Judy, who now live in Arkansas, visited him in Minneapolis. He told them about the conflict, saying that even though it was breaking his heart, he could not agree to getting married. He was surprised by their response:

> I thought they would be moved by my unbending support for them and against institutional homophobia. I was wrong. After [I] explain[ed] the whole situation, my mom said, "I think you should get married!" They told me they thought marriage was a beautiful and important thing. They told me they would support me in finding my own rules and roles in marriage. And they told me that it was not important enough to lose someone you love over it.

With his parents' blessing, Darius was able to tell his partner he was ready to get married. Since then, he has not lost touch with his heritage, as he and his partner have relocated to Northampton—a town in western Massachusetts recognized nationally as "Lesbianville, USA." "I am so happy in my marriage," Darius says. "I look forward to the time that everyone will be able to be included."

As in Darius's family, children benefit from their parents' support as they discover for themselves ways to redefine heterosexual relationships. Parents can assure their children that being in an opposite-sex relationship does not mean they have to abandon their own family's values.

RAISING HETEROSEXUAL CHILDREN WITHOUT SHAME

When heterosexual children become aware of their sexual orientation, some make a point to officially "come out" to their parents in a way that parallels a person coming out as gay. Some parents think it is pretty amusing, but the children who do this are not joking. Other parents are touched by their children's sincerity. These children have thought about it seriously, and they want to be as honest about their sexuality as other people in their community have been about theirs. While most people with straight parents assume that they will be heterosexual, these children are "coming out" as straight because they have reached this conclusion on their own, not because of a heterosexist assumption.

Children need reassurance that their parents' love and support will be unconditional regardless of their own sexual orientation. If one sibling in a family comes out as gay, it is, of course, important for parents to support and celebrate that child's coming-out. But if there are other children in the family, comments and jokes that encourage a "gay vs. straight" division could add to anxiety for children who remain undeclared. If the celebration includes parents saying things like "now you're *really* one of us," the children could interpret it to mean that only the gay children will be fully accepted.

When straight children express anxiety or sadness about their perception of being treated differently in the LGBT community because they are straight, they need their parents to validate those feelings. In a society defined by heterosexuality, it is understandably difficult for parents to comprehend that any person would feel isolated as a result of being straight. Trivializing those feelings, however, will only add to their children's sense of isolation.

It is also critical for LGBT parents to pay attention to the way they talk about heterosexuals and avoid making sweeping generalizations. It is easy to express frustration or anger after a run-in with homophobia by saying, "Why do straight people have to make our lives so difficult?" Presumably, the statement does not apply to every straight person, but a third-grader who overhears will not understand the distinction.

Homophobic *actions* need to be distinguished from heterosexual *identity*. If an issue involving someone being homophobic must be discussed in the presence of children, parents need to focus on the *behavior* that makes the person homophobic. Otherwise, kids conclude that simply *being* heterosexual is what makes someone homophobic. Children can benefit from hearing their parents acknowledge the efforts of straight allies in their community. They need to know that it is possible to build alliances with some straight people, all of whom are not homo-hostile oppressors.

For LGBT people, raising children sometimes involves stepping outside of their own comfort zone in order to provide the support their children need. For example, because gay men are still subjected to the grossly inaccurate stereotype that they are pedophiles, some gay dads are afraid that any parent-child conversation about sex and sexuality could be deemed inappropriate. To safely prevent such an accusation, dads may avoid having that type of conversation altogether. Orson wishes he could have asked his gay dad questions about sex as he was growing up. He didn't get any cues from his dad that those conversations would be welcomed:

> I don't think he was particularly interested in my heterosexual inclinations or interests. There's this sense for a son that you want a father who can talk to you about sex, about dating, and sort of give you advice. And I just never found that he was particularly interested in that part of my life. He didn't ask about if I was dating anybody. Never asked if I was having sex or if I had any questions.

Parents are not always able to meet all of their children's needs. Asking for help from other adults does not mean they are inadequate parents, but some worry that it will appear that way. All parents need help at various times, but those who are sensitive to criticism fear that getting help from outside sources is equivalent to admitting failure. The important thing, however, is that parents are able to recognize when their children's needs could be met with additional help from a mentor, relative, or neighbor.

Jesse wanted to pursue sports like the other boys at school, but he was discouraged by his lesbian parents' lack of enthusiasm. He says his parents were in a "defensive posture" for much of his childhood, which prevented them from asking people outside of their family for help, even when they themselves could not fully nurture his interests. Jesse says:

> Now I see how their feelings about masculinity affected me. They felt an ambivalence toward competitiveness. They didn't want to support what they would consider messed-up masculine roles. I think they saw [sports] as encouraging a patriarchy. They didn't understand how to help me or to acknowledge that that was the world I was in—they didn't know what it was about. It felt like they were setting me up to fail. . . . They didn't think to go outside of their group, or that they could facilitate some sort of low-key interaction with guys that would just be part of a well-rounded childhood.

Many straight adult children wish they could have spent quality time with heterosexual people—male and female—whom their parents respected and trusted. It is contact with people outside the immediate family circle that can foster positive impressions about straight people. Actively seeking out heterosexual role models might seem ridiculous from a gay perspective since heterosexuality is everywhere.

But children do not need to see more heterosexuals in general; they need to see *positive* heterosexual role models, with encouragement from their parents to pursue those relationships.

Looking Forward: Integration or Rejection?

While visiting Provincetown for "Family Week" one summer, I was invited by a lesbian couple and their two college-aged daughters to join them at the women-only beach. A few blankets over, two women were giggling as two little boys, presumably their sons, ran circles around them until they ran out of breath and flopped down on the sand. I wondered how many more years those boys would be able to play on the beach without women complaining that men were in their midst. Later that week, I posed the same question to LGBT parents in my workshop on queer heritage.

That night at an all-family celebration, a single mother from the workshop told me she had been thinking about what I had said regarding the integration of children into the community. "I was at the beach today with my little boy," she said, "and I saw a young man and woman holding hands. At first I was annoyed, thinking, 'What are those straight people doing here?' And then I caught myself and thought, 'Wait a minute. . . . I don't know their story. They could be *ours*.'" She emphasized "ours" with a wide sweeping gesture to include any one of the LGBT parents around her.

The realization that she was raising a child who might grow up to be heterosexual caused a shift in her thinking about how her community should be defined. For her, the separation from straight people has brought a sense of belonging and pride over the years. She now understands that the integration of straight people is what will bring a sense of belonging and pride to her son.

The question of where heterosexual adult children fit into the landscape of LGBT communities will become even more pressing as their numbers grow. Of course, parents hardly have time to ponder the future of their children's identity politics; the focus of parenting is on the present: diapers, car pools, and curfews. Yet, if these issues are not thoughtfully examined now, in ten to fifteen years their kids will experience more extreme culture shock than what today's grown children face. Most of the grown children up to this point were born into a heterosexual marriage, and therefore have a direct connection to straight culture through their straight parent. The "gayby boom" children have two moms, two dads, or one of a combination of numerous queer parents. More parents are choosing to immerse their families in queer communities as much as they can, from neighborhoods to churches to play groups to schools. Parents need to be cognizant of how this intentionally queer upbringing influences, and at times skews, children's perception of heterosexuality.

As the gayby boom and the generations that follow reach adulthood, more children of LGBT parents will consider the LGBT community to be their home, regardless of their sexual orientation. They will push the boundaries of "community" and test the definition of "queer." Ashley Harness, 20, was born in the early years of the gayby boom and is now involved in organizing on her college campus. She explains why including children of LGBT parents is so important:

> I struggle as a queer activist to carve out a place for queerspawn in queer communities. . . . Many of us come from communities in which the definitions of gender and sexuality are far more fluid than those of mainstream America. We are queer by birthright. We *are* the change in our nation that queer communities strive to make through activism. But you must make room for us to be your legacy—to be that change.

As more adult children talk openly about the gifts and challenges that come from their bicultural identities, they provide opportunities for queer communities to look at the impact of defining queerness as beyond "what you do in bed." Children who once wondered if they were being overly dramatic in their quest for belonging now know they are a part of something bigger that validates their previously unarticulated feelings. As Jon wrote when he first contacted me, "I finally know what the hell is 'wrong' with me. I'm a culturally queer man trapped in a straight man's body."

For straight children of LGBT parents who have often wondered what was "wrong" with them, discovering their shared—yet very diverse—identity of being "culturally queer, erotically straight" is a welcome relief. "I'd say it's something about sensibility," Noel Black, 30, says about his common bond with other adult children, "a permission or something, to embrace this familial culture. And there is a definite culture to queerness that was always so private. So I guess it's just the pleasure of having a secret you're no longer hiding."

Facing adulthood and "coming out" as heterosexual does not mean children should have to relinquish ties to the LGBT community—the very community that has loved and nurtured them. If straight children have permission to maintain their sense of belonging, they can proudly carry the gifts of their queer heritage with them into adulthood. They need reassurance that regardless of their sexual orientation, the community that raised them will always be their home.

Epilogue:
In Celebration of
Community

"We have a lot to celebrate," Alysia said, smiling as she raised her glass to clink with the rest. On the eve of New York City's Pride weekend in 2003, eight adult children gathered in a Brooklyn apartment. We toasted to our common bond.

Exactly five years earlier I had wandered alone through the Twin Cities Pride Festival in my homemade T-shirt that proclaimed SOME OF MY BEST PARENTS ARE GAY. As I looked around the table at these friends—some of whom I was meeting in person for the first time—I realized that I now have the connections I once craved.

By coincidence, we were also celebrating the Supreme Court's ruling on *Lawrence v. Texas* the day before. As grown sons and daughters, we all understood the importance of this decision, which removed a major barrier to future rights for LGBT people and their families. It gives us hope for a more safe and just future for children growing up with LGBT parents, and for children in generations to come.

In the twenty-five years since my family first earned its "nontraditional" label, society has shifted significantly, becoming more accepting. I can only imagine how different my childhood would have been if there had been a gay-straight alliance at my school, or if my church had made a point of being "open and affirming," or if I had seen LGBT families represented in the media. Changes that were once unimaginable to me are now realities that make the world a more supportive one for children with LGBT parents.

Despite these encouraging legal and social advances, there is still a long way to go before full equality and acceptance is realized. Every gain is vulnerable to backlash. The *Lawrence* decision, for example, galvanized conservatives to push for amending the U.S. Constitution to define marriage as being solely between a man and a woman. The realities of discrimination, rejection, and heartbreak that LGBT people and their families continue to face prevent me from becoming complacent.

This book emerged from my own silence. When I began speaking out publicly, I did not know if anyone would listen, or if they would even care. Through e-mails, letters, phone calls, handshakes, and hugs, I have the privilege of knowing that my story shares more common ground with other people than I could have ever imagined. I always welcome your comments and questions. My cyber door remains open at www.FamiliesLikeMine.com.

Queer activists often say that grown children of LGBT parents will someday change the world. But we do not have to wait for "someday" because it is already happening. Motivated by their experiences of growing up in queer families, countless adult sons and daughters contribute to changing the world every day. They are teachers who prioritize making their schools safe. They are lawyers who can argue against homophobia in custody cases. Some are journalists who advocate for stories on queer issues that are free from homophobic bias. Others are television producers who introduce queer story lines into mainstream programs. Some are leaders at social service agencies who champion culturally competent programs for queer families. They are doctors, therapists, and professors. Some are parents who are raising their own children in families where differences are respected and everyone is cherished.

On a clear Friday evening last summer, I happened to be driving in Dad and Russ's neighborhood. I decided to drop in and say hello, as I often do. When I parked in front of the house, I could see Dad and Russ in the living room through the big picture window that faces the street. They were sitting on the couch, Russ reading the newspaper and Dad reviewing some documents for work. As I walked up the sidewalk, Dad peered out over his reading specs to look out the window and then waved for me to come inside. The scene made me think about the images of deviant, immoral homosexuals that homo-hostile people cultivate. They sure would be disappointed to observe these two homosexuals in their natural habitat.

The anti-gay rhetoric maintains that growing up in families like mine is confusing to children. It can, at times, be confusing, but not in the way people might assume. After twenty-five years of living in a gay family, I still cannot figure out why upholders of "traditional" family values find us so threatening. *That's* why I'm confused.

But the reasons that homo-hostile people think children of LGBT parents will be confused are much different from mine. They think the root of the confusion will be our inability to conform to rigid ideas of sexuality and gender.

It could be that people who are homo-hostile are the ones who are most confused, since upholding traditional norms as the ideal is becoming more and more of a challenge. The long-term impact of a growing population of people with fluid ideas of gender and sexuality involves asking questions that defenders of so-called family values don't want to consider. What will a future look like in which adults value partnerships over traditional marriages? Or a future in which more men love ballet and more women love power tools? Or a future in which parenting is an assumption for no one, but a choice for everyone?

Does having LGBT parents make a difference in how the kids turn out? Yes, and being raised in families that nurture open-mindedness and acceptance is a wonderful thing. Does being different make it difficult to grow up in these families? Sometimes, but that's because so many people in our society are not yet prepared to entertain life's endless possibilities. Homo-hostile social conservatives feel more secure in their narrow definition of how people "ought" to be. Children of LGBT parents, however, are thriving in this world of possibilities.

No need to worry; it's an exciting place to be.

Appendix A
Queer Cultural Brainstorm

Queer culture influences many parts of life outside of sexual behavior, and regardless of their own sexual orientation, sons and daughters of LGBT parents are affected by its influence. This exercise addresses the question "What is queer culture and what kind of influence might it have on my children?" It is intended to supplement Chapter Eight and will make little sense independent from it.

The brainstorm helps parents and their children identify cultural factors that are unique to their queer culture. (These categories, however, can be used to identify commonalities within *any* community.) In the left column, I included a few examples from my own experience of being in a predominantly gay male environment. That does not mean that all or any of these cultural factors apply to other people with gay parents, but in my experiences talking with other children of gay dads, many of them do. There are additional examples that I mention in Chapter Eight, as well as examples that other sons and daughters mention throughout. The left column would contain different information if I had grown up with more influence from lesbian, transgender, or bisexual cultures. Of course, answers will vary based on geography, religion, socioeconomics, ethnicity, and the era in which the children grew up.

Think about what factors from queer culture are in your life and list them in the column on the right. You can put this away for a few days and come back to it, since you might want to add more after you have had the chance to think about it. Each factor alone might seem minor, but when they are pulled together, they illustrate the fuller picture of queer culture in which sons and daughters are growing up.

The completed form can be shared with other family members to start a conversation about being culturally queer. Here are a few questions to consider:

How do your answers differ from your children's or from your partner's?

What factors in the grid would they remove? What would they add?

What don't they like about queer culture? What are their favorite parts?

Are there times when it is difficult to be culturally queer?

What do sons and daughters want their parents to understand about being culturally queer?

Queer Cultural Brainstorm

Cultural Factor	Examples from Gay Culture (1970s and 1980s)	What factors from LGBT cultures are present in your family?
Language/Code	Dropping code words in front of strangers to confirm they are also "family" Switching pronouns in public "Queer" as a derogatory word	

Entertainment	Musicals: *Company,*
	    A Chorus Line, Cats
	Drag shows and other
	    campy entertainment	

Community	Gay Men's Chorus Gay-owned bookstores Queer coffeehouses Pride festivals	
Food	Appreciation of gourmet food Long hours of preparation Swapping detailed stories of memorable meals	

Values	Pulling together and taking care of
	    our own (impact of AIDS)
	Buying services and goods within
	    gay community
	Distrust in law enforcement
	Family of choice	

Sexuality	No public display of affection Vigilant safer sex	
History	Stonewall Anita Bryant Harvey Milk AIDS	

Appendix B
LGBT Family Resources

Author's Note: Originally quite limited, resources for LGBT families have been growing significantly in recent years. Below are just some of the organizations, films, and books available to families that want to network, find support, and see their lives reflected. I continue to add to the listings on my website, www.FamiliesLikeMine.com. Visitors to the site can sign up for my newsletter which regularly features selected books, links, and other resources.

ORGANIZATIONS

Alternative Family Matters
P.O. Box 390618
Cambridge, MA 02139
Phone: 617-576-6788
Website: www.alternativefamilies.org

COLAGE
(Children of Lesbians and Gays Everywhere)
3543 18th Street, #1
San Francisco, CA 94110
Phone: 415-861-5437
Website: www.colage.org

GLAAD
(Gay & Lesbian Alliance Against Defamation)
248 West 35th Street, 8th floor
New York, NY 10001
Phone: 212-629-3322
Website: www.glaad.org

PFLAG
(Parents, Families and Friends of Lesbians and Gays)
1726 M Street NW, Suite 400
Washington, DC 20036
Phone: 202-467-8180
Website: www.pflag.org

Soulforce, Inc.
(interfaith movement to end spiritual violence)
P.O. Box 3195
Lynchburg, VA 24503-0195
Phone: 877-705-6393
Website: www.soulforce.org

Family Pride Coalition
(for LGBT parents and their families)
P.O. Box 65327
Washington, DC 20035-5327
Phone: 202-331-5015
Website: www.familypride.org

GLSEN
(Gay, Lesbian, and Straight Education Network)
121 West 27th Street, Suite 804
New York, NY 10001-6207
Phone: 212-727-0135
Website: www.glsen.org

Rainbow Families
(serving LGBT families in the Midwest and beyond)
711 West Lake Street, Suite 210
Minneapolis, MN 55408
Phone: 612-827-7731
Website: www.rainbowfamilies.org

FamilyNet—Human Rights Campaign
1640 Rhode Island Avenue NW
Washington, DC 20036-3278
Phone: 202-628-4160
Website: www.hrc.org/familynet

Lambda Legal
120 Wall Street, Suite 1500
New York, NY 10005-3904
Phone: 212-809-8585
Website: www.lambdalegal.org

National Center for Lesbian Rights
870 Market Street, Suite 570
San Francisco, CA 94102
Phone: 415-392-6257
Website: www.nclrights.org

Straight Spouse Network
8215 Terrace Drive
El Cerrito, CA 94530-3058
Phone: 510-525-0200
Website: www.ssnetwk.org

FILM

Daddy and Papa. Dir. Johnny Symons, 2002.
(www.daddyandpapa.com)

It's Elementary: Talking About Gay Issues in School. Dir. Debra
Chasnoff, 1996. (www.womedia.org)

*Our House: A Very Real Documentary About Kids of Gay and Lesbian
Parents*. Dir. Meema Spadola, 1999. (www.colage.org/documentary)

No Dumb Questions. Dir. Melissa Regan, 2001.
(www.nodumbquestions.com)

That's a Family!: A Film for Kids About Family Diversity. Dir. Debra
Chasnoff, 2000. (www.womedia.org)

BOOKS FOR ADULTS

Brill, Stephanie, and Kim Toevs. *The Essential Guide to Lesbian Conception, Pregnancy and Birth.* Los Angeles: Alyson, 2002.

Buxton, Amity Pierce. *The Other Side of the Closet: The Coming-Out Crisis for Straight Spouses and Families.* New York: John Wiley, 1994.

Casper, Virginia, and Steven B. Schultz. *Gay Parents/Straight Schools: Building Communication and Trust.* Williston, Vt.: Teacher's College Press, 1999.

Gillespie, Peggy, ed., and Gigi Kaeser, photographer. *Love Makes a Family: Portraits of Lesbian, Gay, Bisexual, and Transgender Parents and their Families.* Amherst: University of Massachusetts Press, 1999. (The photo exhibit is also on-line: ww.lovemakesafamily.org)

Golombok, Susan, and Fiona L. Tasker. *Growing Up in a Lesbian Family: Effects on Child Development.* New York: Guilford, 1997.

Grever, Carol. *My Husband Is Gay: A Woman's Guide to Surviving the Crisis.* Freedom, Calif.: Crossing Press, 2001.

Howey, Noelle. *Dress Codes: Of Three Girlhoods—My Mother's, My Father's, and Mine.* New York: St. Martin's Press, 2002.

Howey, Noelle, and Ellen Samuels, eds. *Out of the Ordinary: Essays on Growing Up with Gay, Lesbian, and Transgender Parents.* New York: St. Martin's Press, 2000.

Johnson, Susan M., and Elizabeth O'Connor. *For Lesbian Parents: Your Guide to Helping Your Family Grow Up Happy, Healthy and Proud.* New York: Guilford, 2001.

Seyda, Barbara. *Women in Love: Portraits of Lesbian Mothers and Their Families.* Boston: Little, Brown, 1998.

Strah, David, with Susanna Margolis. *Gay Dads: A Celebration of Fatherhood.* New York: Tarcher/Putnam, 2003.

Wells, Jess. ed. *Homefronts: Controversies in Nontraditional Parenting.* Los Angeles, Alyson, 2000.

BOOKS FOR CHILDREN

Atkins, Jeannine. *A Name on the Quilt: A Story of Remembrance.* New York: Simon & Schuster, 1999.*

Combs, Bobbie. *ABC: A Family Alphabet Book.* Ridley Park, Pa.: Two Lives Publishing, 2001.

———. *123: A Family Counting Book.* Ridley Park, Pa.: Two Lives Publishing, 2001.

Elwin, Rosamund. *Asha's Mums.* Toronto: Women's Press, 1990.

Greenberg, Keith. *Zack's Story: Growing Up with Same-Sex Parents.* Minneapolis: Lerner Publications, 1996.

Harris, Robie. *It's So Amazing! A Book About Eggs, Sperm, Birth, Babies, and Families.* Cambridge, Mass.: Candlewick Press, 1999.

Jordan, MaryKate. *Losing Uncle Tim.* Burlington, Vt.: Waterfront, 1989.*

Newman, Lesléa. *Heather Has Two Mommies,* 10th anniversary edition. Los Angeles: Alyson, 2000.

———. *Too Far Away to Touch.* New York, Clarion, 1995.*

Vigna, Judith. *My Two Uncles.* Morton Grove, Ill.: Albert Whitman, 1995.

Willhoite, Michael. *Daddy's Roommate.* Los Angeles: Alyson, 1990.

FICTION FOR YOUNG ADULTS

Bechard, Margaret. *If It Doesn't Kill You.* New York: Viking, 1999.

Garden, Nancy. *Holly's Secret.* New York: Farrar, Straus & Giroux, 2000.

Gleitzman, Morris. *Two Weeks with the Queen.* New York: Putnam, 1991.*

Homes, A. M. *Jack.* New York: Vintage, 1990.

Lowell, Jax Peters. *Mothers.* New York: St. Martin's Press, 1998.

Woodson, Jacqueline. *From the Notebooks of Melanin Sun.* New York: Scholastic, 1995.

* Story line includes AIDS.

Notes

1.   To estimate this population, researchers first must answer two complex societal questions: how is sexual orientation defined, and what constitutes a parent. Differing interpretations of these fundamental issues result in a wide range of estimates. Rationale for the various estimates is outlined in detail in: Patterson, Charlotte J., and Lisa V. Freil, "Sexual Orientation and Fertility." *Infertility in the Modern World: Present and Future Prospects,* edited by G. Bentley and N. Mascie-Taylor. England: Cambridge University Press, 2000.

2.   Simmons, Tavia, and Martin O'Connell, "Married-Couple and Unmarried-Partner Households: 2000." U.S. Census Bureau, Washington, D.C., www.census.gov, February 2003. p. 10. (Based on 301,026 male couples and 293,365 female couples.)

3.   "Considerations Regarding Proposals to Give Legal Recognition to Unions Between Homosexual Persons." Congregation for the Doctrine of the Faith, www.vatican.va, 31 July 2003.

4.   GLAAD 2002 Annual Report, p. 24. The *Primetime Thursday* special "Rosie's Story: For the Sake of the Children" aired on ABC, 14 March 2002, 9 P.M.

5.   Biblarz, Timothy J., and Judith Stacey, "(How) Does the Sexual Orientation of Parents Matter?" *American Sociological Review* 66 (April 2001): 159–183.

6.   Johnson, Susan M., and Elizabeth O'Connor, *For Lesbian Parents: Your Guide to Helping Your Family Grow Up Happy, Healthy and Proud.* New York: Guilford, 2001, p. 158.

7.   Battle, J., C. Cohen, D. Warren, G. Fergerson, and S. Audam, *Say It Loud: I'm Black and I'm Proud: Black Pride Survey 2000.* New York: The Policy Institute of the National Gay and Lesbian Task Force, 2002, pp. 13–14. Survey collected data from 2,645 individuals at Black Pride celebrations in nine U.S. cities.

8.   Quotes from Howey are from an interview conducted by Garner that originally aired on KFAI, 2 May 2002.

9.   Rawls, Phillip, "Chief Justice Says Homosexuals Unfit as Parents." Associated Press, 15 February 2002.

10.   The Gay & Lesbian Advocates & Defenders. "Protecting Families: Standards of Child Custody in Same-Sex Relationships," Boston, 1999, p. 3. The document was drafted in collaboration with Lambda Legal, National Center for Lesbian Rights, Family Pride Coalition, and the American Civil Liberties Union Lesbian and Gay Rights Project, and is endorsed by COLAGE. It is available on GLAD's website, www.glad.org/Publications/CivilRightProject/protectingfamilies.pdf, as well as on the collaborators' websites.

11.   Johnson, Wanda Y., *Youth Suicide: The School's Role in Prevention and Response*. Bloomington, Ind.: Phi Delta Kappa Educational Foundation, 1999, pp. 47–49.

12.   An Australian study of thirty-eight students with gay and lesbian parents showed that many of their experiences with bullies in school mirrored the experiences of queer youth. The study was published in: Ray, Vivien, and Robin Gregory, "School Experiences of the Children of Lesbian and Gay Parents." *Family Matters* 59 (winter 2001): 28–34. Comparable studies done in the United States that are specific to children of LGBT parents in schools have not been published.

13.   Cowley, Geoffrey, "Our Bodies, Our Fears." *Newsweek*, 24 February 2003. p. 48.

14.   McIntosh, Peggy, *White Privilege and Male Privilege: A Personal Account of Coming to See Correspondences Through Work in Women's Studies*. Working Paper No. 189, Wellesley College Center for Research on Women. Wellesley, Mass., 1988. p. 7.

15.   Ibid., p. 17.

16.   As of the publication of this book, the following states ban employment discrimination based on sexual orientation extending to the public and private sector: California, Connecticut, Hawaii, Maryland, Massachusetts, Minnesota, Nevada, New Hampshire, New Jersey, New Mexico, New York, Rhode Island, Vermont, Wisconsin, and the District of Columbia. Only four states prohibit discrimination based on gender identity: California, Minnesota, New Mexico, and Rhode Island.

17.   Centers for Disease Control and Prevention, "Need for Sustained HIV Prevention Among Men Who Have Sex with Men." MSM Fact Sheet, May 2002. www.cdc.gov/hiv/pubs/facts/msm.pdf

18.   Yee, Daniel, "CDC Says New HIV Cases Rose in 2002." Associated Press, 29 July 2003. Statistics are based on data from twenty-five states in the United States.

19.   Centers for Disease Control and Prevention, "Need for Sustained HIV Prevention . . ."

20.   Some readers might be more familiar with the term "safe sex" when referring to the use of condoms or other barriers that reduce the risk of transmission of HIV and sexuality transmitted diseases. "Safer sex," however, is the term preferred by many health educators, because it emphasizes that there are many ways to make sex safer, but that no sexual practice is guaranteed to be 100 percent "safe."

21.   Biblarz and Stacey, p. 170: ". . . parental influence on children's sexual desires is neither direct nor easily predictable."

22.   Stockman, Farah, "July 4th Assault on Woman Eyed as Antigay Hate Crime." *Boston Globe,* 12 July 2003.

23.   Patton, Clarence, *Anti-Lesbian, Gay, Bisexual and Transgender Violence in 2002.* National Coalition of Anti-Violence Programs. New York, 2003, p. 4.

Acknowledgments

This book is a culmination of eight years of community organizing and activism. I am grateful to so many people whose paths have crossed with mine. I will try my best to name as many of them as possible.

I owe big thanks to the people whom I interviewed specifically for this book, both those who were included in the final draft and those who were not. It has been a joy getting to know so many of my peers; I am proud to be among you.

Before I had decided to limit the scope of the book to adult children, my more general query for participants brought me nearly three hundred responses from LGBT parents. Thank you to all the families who volunteered so eagerly; I hope to reconnect with many of you for future projects.

I am grateful to my agent, Joy E. Tutela, who helped me revive this dream which had been languishing on the back burner. Thanks also to my editor at HarperCollins, Gail Winston, who brought clarity and direction to the project. Together, Joy and Gail have been a terrific team, frequently invigorating me with an extra dose of enthusiasm. Thanks also to Gail's fabulous assistant, Christine Walsh, who kept the logistics moving along smoothly.

Other key players who saw to it that I completed this project were: Glenn Shope, a dear friend and cohort who is also a great coach; Marshall Miller, who served as my "book doula" with his trademark compassion; and Sofia T. Romero, who has been my always-on-call editor since college and also my best friend. Additional friends who lent a hand while I worked on this project include: Kathy Klar and Orion Petersen, Nicole Pettit, and Eric P. Strauss. Thanks also to Echo and Tom, my house sitters extraordinaire when I am on the road.

I am grateful to everyone who agreed to read drafts of various chapters. They loaned me their smarts and sensibilities to provide valuable feedback that helped me shape and rework this book. Those readers were: Alysia Abbott, Caitlin Baldwin, Amity Pierce Buxton, Dan Cherubin, Tina Fakhrid-Deen, Jenifer Firestone, Jim Foti, Kelly Griffith, Ashley Harness, Rosanne Johnson, Kristin E. Joos, Bronwyn Leebaw, Daniel Lessem, Stefan Lynch, DeAnna Miller, Marshall Miller, John Quinlan, Sofia T. Romero, Laura Smidzik, and Betty Tisel.

Thanks to Peggy Drexler, Anndee Hochman, Charlotte Patterson, and Judith Stacey, for making sure that copies of their work were readily accessible to me. Also helpful in responding to my questions were Lisa Bennett, Corri Planck, Alice Ruby, and Gail Taylor. Thanks to everyone at the all-volunteer Quatrefoil Library, an oasis of information on all things queer. Additional research assistance was provided by Ashley Harness and Kristin E. Joos. Thanks to Nancy Silverrod from the San Francisco Public Library, who shared her expertise on LGBT literature for young people; many of her suggestions appear in Appendix B. I am also indebted to Aleta Fenceroy and Jean Mayberry, who continually reinforce the maxim "knowledge is power."

I extend my warm appreciation to the dedicated staff and volunteers across the country who work with COLAGE, Family Pride Coalition, PFLAG, Straight Spouse Network, and Rainbow Families to advocate on behalf of LGBT families. Thank you, each and every one of you. I know that much of the work is not glamorous, but all of it matters. I am also grateful to the people who served on a certain steering committee which later grew to become COLAGE. Those pioneers included: Emily Gmerek Hache, Anna Heller, Molly Heller, Hope Berry Manley, and Ali Nickel-Dubin.

There have been countless fellow writers, community leaders, colleagues, and friends who were there for me at just that right moment to show me how to connect the dots, or encourage me out of a slump, or welcome me in unfamiliar territory. Just some of the people who I want to thank include: Chris Beccone, Kit Briem, Laurie Buss, Amber Davis, Florence Dillon, Michael Downing, Scott Fearing, Jenifer Firestone, Jill G., Jon and Michael Galluccio, Candace Gingrich, Sue Grieger, Ernie Gonzalez, Kathryn H., Sarah B. Harris, Noelle Howey, Sal Iacullo and Wayne Steinman, Joyce Kauffman, Douglas "DK" Kearney, Rob Keeling, Sol Kelley-Jones, Jude Koski and Carolyn Laub, Deanna Lackaff, Stephen Lander, Brian Malloy, Nick Metcalf, Molly Peacock, Kirk Read, Cathy Renna, Martha Roth, Barbara Satin, Seth Saturn, Meema Spadola, Joni Thome, David K. Wells III, and so many others, including everyone who has ever said to me, "You should write a book."

I also want to thank Amy Lindgren, whose class on writing a column gave me the excuse to finally get something down on paper. Rudy Renaud was the first editor to run the column, giving me two years to try out many of the ideas that appear in this book. Thanks also to Susan Perry, for her course on how to write a book proposal. I am also grateful to the wonderful staff at the Loft Literary Center, where I wrote most of this manuscript. My anthropology professor at Wellesley College, Sally Engle Merry, introduced me to the notion of culture which helped me make sense of my heritage. My mentor, Jean Kilbourne, showed me through her own example how a woman could turn her life's passion into her life's work.

Mom, Dad, and Russ deserve heaps of love and gratitude for sitting back with open hearts as they watch this journey unfold. When they first gave me their blessing to talk publicly about our family, we had no concept of the potential size of my audience. It is no small thing for them to support me as I examine our private family in such public ways.

Extra special thanks goes to my mother, who rallied graciously in the final days before deadline to keep me fed, caffeinated, and focused. It was just like the days when she coached me through high school research papers and college applications. Fortunately, this time there were no tantrums or tears.

Index

women-only space, sons in, 20–21,
    203–5, 222
women's health cooperatives, 151–52
www.FamiliesLikeMine.com, 226

www.steaveabbott.org, 166. *See also* Abbott, Alysia

Yates, Andrea, 26